Inventions in Fashion
From Rawhide to Rayon

Lisa Hiton

New York

Published in 2017 by Cavendish Square Publishing, LLC
243 5th Avenue, Suite 136, New York, NY 10016

Copyright © 2017 by Cavendish Square Publishing, LLC

First Edition

No part of this publication may be reproduced, stored in a retrieval system, or transmitted in any form or by any means—electronic, mechanical, photocopying, recording, or otherwise—without the prior permission of the copyright owner. Request for permission should be addressed to Permissions, Cavendish Square Publishing, 243 5th Avenue, Suite 136, New York, NY 10016. Tel (877) 980-4450; fax (877) 980-4454.

Website: cavendishsq.com

This publication represents the opinions and views of the author based on his or her personal experience, knowledge, and research. The information in this book serves as a general guide only. The author and publisher have used their best efforts in preparing this book and disclaim liability rising directly or indirectly from the use and application of this book.

CPSIA Compliance Information: Batch #CW17CSQ

All websites were available and accurate when this book was sent to press.

Cataloging-in-Publication Data

Names: Hiton, Lisa.
Title: Inventions in fashion: from rawhide to rayon / Lisa Hiton.
Description: New York : Cavendish Square Publishing, 2017. | Series: Art and invention | Includes index.
Identifiers: ISBN 9781502623058 (library bound) | ISBN 9781502623065 (ebook)
Subjects: LCSH: Fashion--History--Juvenile literature. | Inventions--History--Juvenile literature.
Classification: LCC TT504.H55 2017 | DDC 746.9'2--dc23

Editorial Director: David McNamara
Editor: Caitlyn Miller
Copy Editor: Nathan Heidelberger
Associate Art Director: Amy Greenan
Designer: Joseph Macri
Production Assistant: Karol Szymczuk
Photo Research: J8 Media

The photographs in this book are used by permission and through the courtesy of: Cover Wilawan Khasawong/Alamy Stock Photo; p. 4 A. B. Wenzel/Conde Nast Collection/Getty Images; p. 10 Stock Montage/Archive Photos/Getty Images; pp. 13, 47 Ullstein Bild/Getty Images; p. 16 George Rinhart/Corbis/Getty Images; p. 19 Roberto Brosan/The LIFE Images Collection/Getty Images; p. 23 Independent Picture Service/UIG/Getty Images; p. 26 Photomadn/Alamy Stock Photo; p. 27 Michael Sewell/Photolibrary/Getty Images; p. 33 Craig Tuttle/Corbis Documentary/Getty Images; p. 35 Silver Screen Collection/Archive Photos/Getty Images; pp. 40-41 Richard Levin/Alamy Stock Photo; p. 43 Photos.com/Thinkstock.com; p. 51 AF archive/Alamy Stock Photo; p. 53 NEMPR Picture the Past/Heritage Images/Getty Images; pp. 58-59 Universal History Archive/Getty Images; p. 61 Hulton Archive/Getty Images; p. 67 Anaiz777/iStock/Thintstock.com; p. 68 Wikimedia Commons/Public Domain/Tucker Collection/File:Camille Dreyfus portrait.jpg/PD US; p. 71 Wikimedia Commons/Ben Mills/File:Cellulose-Ibeta-from-xtal-2002-3D-vdW.png/PD; pp. 72-73 Wikimedia Commons/Ben Mills/File:Cellulose-Ibeta-from-xtal-2002-CM-3D-balls.png/PD; pp. 76-77 Artokoloro Quint Lox Limited/Alamy Stock Photo; p. 82 Ethan Miller/Getty Images; p. 85 Moleskine; p. 87 Selcuk Acar/Anadolu Agency/Getty Images; pp. 94-95 Stephen Lovekin/Getty Images for IMG.

Printed in the United States of America

CONTENTS

Introduction: Art You Wear Every Day	5
Chapter 1: The Roots of Modern Fashion Design	9
Chapter 2: Rawhide	25
Chapter 3: Blue Jeans	39
Chapter 4: The Sewing Machine	53
Chapter 5: Rayon	66
Chapter 6: The Future of Fashion	83
Glossary	99
Bibliography	102
Further Information	106
Index	108
About the Author	112

The first issue of *Vogue* magazine was released in 1892.

VOGUE—A DEBUTANTE

INTRODUCTION: Art You Wear Every Day

The arts seek to bring us beauty in many forms. In fact, beauty is often reflected in both the content of art itself and the methods the artist has used to create the content. Fashion, too, demonstrates the importance of process *and* product. But unlike every other art form, fashion is art that you can handle and wear every day. Fashion is not meant to be displayed behind glass in a stuffy museum. Rather, it's art that you interact with every day of your life, no matter who you are or where you're from.

In short, fashion is for the masses. Though there are different genres within fashion, it is an art form that doesn't care about how deep your pockets are. We might not all be able to afford a Louis Vuitton purse, yet we have the freedom to define our own style. Because of this freedom of expression, fashion is as empowering as it is controversial. Over time, the introduction of new technology, designs, fabrics, buttons, and shapes have inspired huge reactions. And as fashions evolve, they take on new meanings in popular culture. For instance, while **leather** jackets were once the uniform of military aviators, they soon became an emblem of cool and resistance to authority.

However, not everyone has the freedom to choose what they wear. Until the late 1800s, women in America didn't wear pants or trousers because of societal conventions.

These conventions still exist today in different forms—some countries even have strict laws about clothing, and many times these laws affect women's freedoms more than those of men. Most schools ban students from wearing clothes that don't meet their standards of appropriateness; other schools remove fashion choices entirely and require their students to wear uniforms.

Despite cultural norms, oppressive governments, and more, fashion has continued to evolve. New inventions and discoveries in textiles and design have furthered the medium. Fashion designers and style icons use the humble act of getting dressed to stand for freedom of individuality.

Nowadays we know fashion to be an art, but it began as something else: utility. Humans are the first species to make and use clothing. The earliest known uses of clothing were meant to serve as protection from the elements. While we still use clothes for this purpose, the style of those clothes signifies much more than basic survival. As time passed from early human civilization, clothes have become markers of attitude, class, ethnicity, gender, and time period. From the introductions of various materials, improvements made to existing materials, and the industrialization of clothing production, we now have a whole new world of fashion. We've gone from those early means of protection and survival to the vast variety of color, material, and pattern.

Industrialization, in fact, signaled a huge change in human civilization. Women were once responsible for making clothing for their families, yet the invention and advancement of machines like the cotton gin and the sewing machine meant that clothing could be mass produced far more quickly than it could be crafted by hand. The mechanization of garment making disrupted the livelihoods of seamstresses and tailors—none of them could out-sew a machine. Throughout the modern era, human civilization often invents a machine that stands to erase a human skill or craft from the world. But humans also learn quickly to adapt to changes and to preserve skills and ideas worth keeping.

The main elements of fashion are design and textiles. We wouldn't have boots without leather. We wouldn't have blue jeans without **denim**. And we'd be nowhere in fashion without the likes of the sewing machine, zippers, buttons, or lace. Behind these objects is industrialization, trade, distribution, and merchandising. While manufacturing keeps the fashion industry moving, artists and inventors continue to find ways to disrupt the market and remind us that style (and innovation!) is in our own hands.

In the beginning of garment making, craftsmen and artists invented tools to make clothes easier to produce than with a simple needle and thread. They also sought out new materials and colors in nature for inspiration in making clothes for utility and, later, for style. From bone needles to the sewing machine, fashion designers and craftsmen alike considered the relationship between clothes, culture, and utility in their works. Now, digital technologies stand to change fashion all over again, offering artists new approaches to unique materials, new ways of designing and producing clothes, and a whole new expansion of style.

While these new materials and ideas pave the way for a new look altogether, the process is not so different for these artists as it was for fashion designers of the past. Innovators in the fashion world, like scientists, go through a process of trial and error. Both fashion designers and the men and women who invented technology that forever changed the landscape of fashion rely on hundreds of years of knowledge when it comes to making clothes. These innovators have to know how clothes are cut, dyed, sewn, and otherwise produced. All kinds of artistic, chemical, and business processes are behind the clothes we wear, and the inventions that have revolutionized fashion often have applications that surpass the runway. Fashion technology is used to produce all kinds of products we use in our everyday lives.

Trends in the market and in fashion have changed many times over the course of history. But style is something we can make all our own. From footwear, to attire, to hats, accessories, and makeup, we have the power to let the science and art of fashion guide our aesthetic choices every day, just like innovators in fashion.

CHAPTER 1
The Roots of Modern Fashion Design

The fashion industry today is made up of many components like manufacturing, retailing, and advertising. Because the fashion industry focuses heavily on these three components, design is often an afterthought in our minds—as well as the minds of large manufacturers. For example, when you walk into a store like Zara, H&M, or Urban Outfitters, who designed the items that you choose to buy? Many companies do not include designers' names on clothing labels. The idea of an artist behind the clothes we wear is mostly found in high fashion or well-established fashion houses.

This phenomenon is actually similar to how things were at the advent of clothing. In the beginning, clothes were meant to protect people from the elements. Design was not nearly as important as function. Early people never would have thought of adding a label crediting an article of clothing's designer. As civilizations progressed, garments were differentiated by materials—the more complex or expensive a material, dye, or button was, the higher your rank in society. From the loincloth to Parisian fashion of the twentieth century, many inventions and discoveries would have to occur for the purpose of clothes to change from utility and survival to style.

To understand the complex factors that make up the fashion world of today, we need to look backward. This

The Champs-Élysées in Paris, depicted in this illustration, is still one of the most significant places for haute couture in the world.

chapter looks at how fashion became the art form we know, thanks largely to the innovations of Parisian fashion houses, before tracing our way back to the role of design and invention at the dawn of man.

RISING FASHION in the WEST

When we hear the word "fashion," many of us will think of Hollywood, New York City, Paris, and Milan. This high fashion (also known as haute couture) gives us art pieces on the runway, converted to expensive, well-made clothes for the elite. The difference between clothes for the masses and the idea that clothes could make a larger cultural statement was born in Paris at the turn of the twentieth century.

In fact, many early figures in fashion come from Paris. There's a good reason that Paris remains the world's fashion capital: the city is the birthplace of haute couture. Haute couture represents a significant turning point in fashion. High fashion values quality over quantity and beauty over utility. While fashion trends fluctuate between these ideals, great artists like Charles Worth, Paul Poiret, and Coco Chanel were truly groundbreaking figures in haute couture.

Charles Worth

Charles Worth was an Englishman who moved to Paris in 1845 in an effort to become a great fashion designer—a couturier. Worth was inspired by historic portraits he'd seen in museums; this inspiration is obvious in his dress designs.

Worth began his career in fashion working for a textile company in Paris. Eventually his work in sales led him to opening a small dressmaking division within the company. His work won prizes and was exhibited at the Great Exhibition of London and the Exposition Universalle in Paris. His success allowed him to branch out on his own.

In 1858, Worth opened the first haute couture fashion house in Paris, the House of Worth. At this time, the establishment of the Second Empire in France was the perfect pairing for Worth's artistic ambitions. His lavish taste reflected the revitalized economic state of the country. Worth made custom dresses for members of high society and was also known for putting his dresses on live models at the House of Worth so clients could see his designs before the custom tailoring process began.

Worth's rise to fame was rapid. Not only was he well known by the upper crust, but his status as the "father of haute couture" meant that his name appeared in fashion magazines for the masses. Women from every town in France knew his work, even if they'd never be able to afford his clothing themselves.

Worth dominated Parisian fashion for the whole of his career. His two sons took over the business after he died in 1895 at the age of seventy. His sons continued Worth's aesthetic—lavish fabrics and trimmings—keeping the House of Worth thriving through the 1920s (another era known for its haute couture). The House of Worth ended when his great-grandson retired from the family business.

Paul Poiret

In the early 1900s, fashion saw a new revolutionary in the arrogant and charming Paul Poiret. Poiret opened a haute couture fashion house in 1903. Poiret had first apprenticed at the House of Worth, where he was to make the "side" garments to accompany Worth's elaborate works. Striking off on his own, he instantly became notorious: in America, he was "the King of Fashion," while in Paris he was known as "*Le Magnifique*" ("The Magnificent"). Poiret drew on

Paul Poiret fits a woman for one of his signature outfits, including harem pants.

diverse inspiration to debut dramatic shapes that fashion in the West had not yet seen. His affinity for Asian culture as well as the Russian ballet led his designs to a new territory of exploration: theater.

Poiret was known for his dramatic silhouettes and use of color. He is perhaps best remembered for iconic designs like the lampshade tunic and harem pants.

Not only were these styles new to Paris, but they undid two longstanding trends in women's fashion: the petticoat and the corset. Women's fashion had been defined by these uncomfortable garments, yet Poiret was after a different look.

Unlike many designers, the young Poiret spent lots of time drawing his designs and shopping the drawings around to potential clients. As a young boy, his parents made him work with an umbrella designer. Poiret would take the silk scraps home and turn them into dresses. This way of thinking helped him visualize fashion in terms of both high culture and usefulness. His pieces spoke to each other, suggesting to the public a cohesiveness that we now recognize as the concept of a fashion line.

Poiret's artistic acumen also changed the skills that went into design. The old way of considering the clothed body required tailoring—a practice in form and fit—yet Poiret's new silhouettes innovated the skill of draping as part of fashion design. The nineteenth century had championed pattern pieces for mass production. Poiret took inspiration from delicately crafted pieces like kimonos, chitons, and caftans instead.

Poiret continued to draw his works with a French stenciling technique known as pochoir, and he published them. Not only was he a successful designer, but he championed the relationship between fashion and art, trying to ensure that relationship would be cemented in fashion history and preserved for future generations of designers and stylists. During and after World War I, Poiret's work perhaps seemed unnecessary to culture at large. The war found many people focusing on day-to-day survival, not ornamental fashion designs. As the cultural landscape underwent drastic change, Paris would need to see a new revolutionary to hold its claim as the world's fashion capital.

Gabrielle "Coco" Chanel

While other couturiers were revolutionizing shapes, honing their business acumen, and forecasting trends, society was on the brink of an even larger shift: a complete reworking of women's fashion. Though Poiret was one major reason that women began abandoning the confining fashions of the former century, many women held on to the fashions of the past. It would take another towering figure to change women's fashion once and for all.

In 1913, on the brink of World War I, Gabrielle "Coco" Chanel opened her first two boutiques: one in Paris and the other in the resort town of Deauville, France. Prior to becoming a fashion designer, Chanel was an impoverished child sent to a convent for school. She rebelled against her upbringing, hoping to become an actress. Staging and costuming helped her become a milliner, or women's hat designer. At her shops, she sold hats and select clothing items. Chanel's style and charm brought her a loyal clientele from the start.

In the interest of saving money while she established herself, Chanel made her garments primarily out of jersey. The fabric was used only to make men's underwear at the time. It was cheap and novel. Chanel's clothes were far more casual than the preceding styles. Although it was affordable, jersey proved to be a quality fabric, and it's one we still use widely these days. Chanel was inspired by more than economic choices, though. The looming war found

Coco Chanel is famous for her many contributions to fashion. Here, she is in a trademark suit and beret.

its way into her designs. Chanel applied aspects of men's uniforms, like their simple, utilitarian shapes, to women's wear. Unlike Worth and Poiret before her, Chanel was not afraid to let go of excess.

When the war broke out, many fled Paris for the outskirts of the city. Luckily, Chanel had shops where these Parisians were heading. Her simple and practical designs did surprisingly well given the circumstances at hand. Chanel was known for her uncluttered style. She shortened women's skirts, allowing women to be more active, especially as women were given more work and responsibilities while young men were away at war. Chanel was famous (financially and societally) by the time she was in her early thirties. Founded by a lone woman among a world of male designers, the House of Chanel still stands as a beacon of grand achievement in the middle of Paris.

Chanel herself was slim with boyish cropped hair. Her own style and way of life gave way to the fashions she created for women. By the 1920s, Chanel's own identity mirrored trending fashions. Women started playing sports, paving the way for freer clothing designs, shorter hair, and more relaxed fabrics. This held true for the more formal evening look of this same woman as a flapper. Zippers, shoulder pads, buttons, and bright pink all entered the fashion world at this time, and Chanel wasn't afraid to use any of these elements.

Chanel was also known for her color palette, which relied heavily on shades of beige, black, and white. It may seem simple now, but next to the bright colors of the House of Worth or "Le Magnifique," Paul Poiret, this color palette turned out to be bold, brash, and forward.

World War II and Paris Fashion

In the 1930s, hemlines dropped, and so did the spirits of many Parisians. Hemlines would rise again, but the

COCO CHANEL'S LEGACY

Chanel created many iconic looks for women through the 1920s. Her most famous, perhaps, was the "little black dress," suitable for day and evening. American *Vogue* likened this innovative design to the Ford—the first car to the race and universally beloved.

Not only was this the birth of the little black dress as a phenomenon, but it was also the introduction of designing clothes for "day to night." Chanel was not only changing fashion but showing the world that she understood the changing pace of life—for women especially. Chanel also invented the first woman's suit, pioneered the use of colorful chiffon, and even created a famous scent, Chanel No. 5, which still exists today.

On a larger scale, Chanel was ahead of the textile and manufacturing industries as well. And Chanel's whole career, all the way until her death in 1971, involved her attitude as part of her art. She is still known as one of the most important arbiters of taste in fashion, nearly half a century after her death.

> Chanel No. 5 was inspired by flappers.

The Roots of Modern Fashion Design 19

fabric of French life would be forever changed. Many Paris fashion houses closed at the onset of World War II. Chanel was one of them. The political climate in 1939 Paris was unsafe, as was the whole of Europe, and really the world. But France was Germany's neighbor, and in 1939, France declared war on Germany. Chanel closed her doors and stayed in Paris, trying to keep life simple during a time of tremendous difficulty.

After the war, a new star rose in Parisian fashion: Christian Dior. Determined to reestablish Paris as the world's fashion capital after a long period of such darkness, Dior launched his first collection, the "New Look," in 1947. His response to years of uniforms (which he wore when he served in World War II) and utility was to turn away from it with extreme femininity. The collection featured cinched waists with full skirts, rounded shoulders, and lavish fabrics. He called his new silhouette the "figure 8," accentuating the womanly shape by exaggerating it. Perhaps his most iconic design was the A-line waist for dresses.

During Dior's emergence, Chanel decided to reopen her doors. Her judgment and taste told her that Dior's efforts to create a "New Look" were backwards. Instead of being modern, Dior's designs had returned to the old tropes with some new bells and whistles. Dior, by Chanel's measure, missed the point entirely: women's lives were new, and what they wore needed to reflect those changes. Dior's desire to abandon the practical ignored the fact that women's roles in societies were fundamentally changed after yet another world war. Chanel would have to come back and rescue women's fashion once again.

Unlike the uber-feminine silhouettes and palette of Dior, Chanel's comeback collections revised her body of work. The results spoke for themselves: her showroom was packed with celebrities and wealthy women. The Chanel suit became the new status symbol for generations of women to come. Her simple, classic touches of solid fabrics, twill, and slim skirts mirrored and progressed the attitudes of the women who wore her clothes.

In order for these visionaries to do their work, they needed to be innovative, radical, and tireless. From working with new fabrics to new dyes, these artists also needed to be keen on technical understanding as much as the understanding of how their clothes made people feel. Fashion's visionaries in Paris also relied on new inventions to help them do their work. The sewing machine, new textiles like denim and rayon, and leather tanneries are huge manufacturing industries that make working with fashion materials possible. And so, while we may think of these iconic fashion images first, without the inventions from early human history to the tanneries of today, we would not have any of fashion's most iconic looks.

FROM PARIS to PREHISTORY

Of course, the major fashion houses in Paris could never produce clothing without the foundations laid by those who came before them. It's hard to imagine, but modern fashion owes a huge debt of gratitude to early man. Without early fabrics or early tools, who knows where fashion would be? In the following sections, we'll explore the textiles and tools that serve as the basis for *all* fashion design throughout history.

Early Textiles

The first known textile during ancient times was likely felt. Silk is another contender for being the first textile, though, as humans observed silkworms spinning it in nature. In most cases, textiles are felted (the process of making the fabric and the fabric itself share the same name) or spun into yarn. With that yarn, humans could knit, loop, or weave garments, blankets, and more. Early clothing was woven on a loom.

As different regions became known for their textiles, trading between nations became a popular means of commerce. Further, creating textiles became an industry that employed weavers, tailors, and seamstresses.

Early Tools

The basic tools needed to create a garment (or anything else made of fabric) are the fabric; thread; needle; and an **awl**, which is used to pierce thick fabrics. Aside from these, basic tools were needed to make cloth itself, like looms and sewing thread.

A loom is a basic machine used to weave cloth and tapestry. There are many kinds of looms throughout human history that help create textiles and cloths. Ancient civilizations mostly used a back strap loom, where yarn or thread is spread between two sticks. Similar to a hammock, one stick is attached to something sturdy, like a tree, while the other stick is attached to a sling worn around the weaver's back. Simply leaning back pulls the device taut. Weavers then make cloth by hand.

Handlooms, draw looms, and other traditional looms were eventually replaced by power looms in the late 1700s. A power loom is a mechanized version of a silk or cotton loom, which was pioneered during the Industrial Revolution.

In more recent centuries, spooled sewing thread was a staple item of every household. Mothers and daughters often used thread to make clothes, sheets, and other necessities for their families.

While many inventions in fashion were patented by men, in 1793, Hannah Wilkinson Slater received a patent for cotton sewing thread that she twisted on her spinning

A back strap loom in action

wheel, making her the first woman in America to receive a patent. Spooled thread of different materials, like cotton and silk, opened new avenues in commerce and sewing. Wilkinson's invention eventually led to embroidery, which laid the foundation of fashion's relationship to style instead of utility. Without Wilkinson's invention, thread might not have become as popular. Perhaps more importantly, the sewing machine may never have come to fruition without spooled thread.

BACK to the BEGINNING

Innovation is important to any art form—it's the part of humans that makes us novel. And yet, no creativity can come without an origin. In the case of fashion, even the most digital of advances still owe so much to what we find in nature. The original materials that helped humans become a dressed species came from surviving in the world: bones became bone needles; animal **hides** became clothing, shoes, and shelter; and even the idea of spooling thread came first from the silkworm.

Fashion is an art especially interested in the culture from which it comes. While the West continues to globalize and manufacture all kinds of clothes, there are still cultures all over the world whose garb represents different values—not just values given based on trade laws, but cultural values. Gauchos (cowboys) of South America need their clothes to endure far more extreme conditions than our school clothes can. Countries with high temperatures need fabrics that breathe and move. All of these factors are represented in the inventions in design and textiles nation by nation, throughout human history.

And as much as things have changed and veered toward expression since Paris at the turn of the century, there are still First Nations peoples producing **rawhide** like their ancestors did to this day. The next chapter takes a closer look at how rawhide clothed early humans and evolved into the leather industry.

CHAPTER 2
Rawhide

Rawhide is one of the oldest materials known to human civilization. The untreated hide of an animal was used for survival: it is a prominent part of early clothing, early armor, insulation, and various early tools. Nowadays, rawhide mostly conjures leather to mind. Unlike rawhide, leather is a processed material. To make leather, the hide of an animal is tanned in a process similar to pickling food. Tanning both preserves and breaks down the material. Though different in feel and strength, these two materials made of animal hides served human communities across many nations and histories.

Rawhide and leather are still used widely (in clothing and furniture) and aren't seen as the trappings of cavemen. In fact, the fabric often inspires nostalgia for the days of the Wild West. Contemporary tanneries across the United States sell everything from belts and boots to couches and beyond.

PRECURSORS to RAWHIDE

Although rawhide seems like something basic, the processes by which rawhide was made have a long history. Rawhide

Stretching a cowhide in the sun dries and shapes it.

was central to human survival. As humans began to travel, hides and furs became part of fur trade movements. At every turn in early history, humans looked to nature for inspired means of weathering the elements. And like the animals seen in a given landscape, hunters made use of anything that could aid their own survival.

Animal Hides

Archaeologists have found evidence of animal hides associated with all instances of *Homo sapiens* since prehistoric times. Hides served as a source of clothing and shelter. One of the oldest examples of cultures that used hides are the Inuits. Inuits are part of the First Nation, live in the Arctic, and have many traditions that use animal hides today.

The Inuits invented the parka—a hooded coat, lined with fur.

PARCHMENT AND VELLUM

During the Iron Age, Pergamon—an ancient Greek city—saw the birth of one of the world's oldest forms of paper: parchment. Parchment paper was made from rawhide. In Greece at that time, papyrus was the reigning paper. Papyrus paper was made from the papyrus plant and first manufactured in ancient Egypt.

Ancient Greek culture led to a boom in writing—from philosophy, to math, to science, Greek thinkers were leading human civilization to its most astute discoveries and teachings. Papyrus was everywhere, letting writers, artists, and poets keep and preserve thoughts.

King Ptolemy (367 BCE–283 BCE) banned papyrus export from Pergamon. He wanted to make sure that Alexandria's library remained Greece's superior house of books. In response to the ban, parchment was developed from rawhide. The word parchment comes from *pergamena* for Pergamon.

Even farther back in time, animal skin was used for writing. The oldest known use takes the form of the scrolls of the Old Testament. The technical word for this paper is vellum. Vellum specifically refers to calfskin (whereas parchment, at the time of its origination, referred explicitly to paper made in Pergamon).

Living in Greenland, northern Canada, and Alaska can be brutal. Imagine trying to survive in such unforgiving landscapes before the advancements of electricity, running water, and protective gear. Hunting was (and still is) a part of life in the wilderness. An animal killed for food came with fur and hide. The Inuits used these parts of the animal for shelter and clothing. Skins were cut and sewn together to make waterproof clothes. Furs were used to protect from the cold. These hides were also used to make tents and kayaks.

Likewise, these uses were seen further south in indigenous American communities. Native Americans used animal hides for teepees, wigwams, moccasins, and buckskins. Hides were also used as drumheads. Native Americans made shields out of rawhide, too.

The INVENTION ITSELF

Rawhides are mostly uncommon these days as hides are prone to rotting, and their texture changes depending on temperature. Mostly, rawhide has led to the leather industry. At their outset, leather materials were made out of necessity, but like many fashion trends, utility turned to aesthetic.

While craftsmen were once the pioneers and champions of leather invention, as fashion and style rose in more recent centuries, fashion designers came to the forefront of keeping the leather business afloat. There are still small pockets of the world where early traditions of rawhide and leather use are still in place, but they are becoming increasingly scarce as technological advancements lead to progress.

The MECHANICS of LEATHER

Unlike rawhide, leather goes through a process, making the properties of the animal skin useful and sustainable in our day-to-day lives. The tanning process is responsible for the advancements made from rawhide to leather, and now to more complex leather manufacturing than ever before.

A hide has three layers: the epidermis, the dermis, and the subcutaneous layer (flesh). The epidermis layer is the outermost part of the skin. Hair and fur are attached here. In leather processing, this layer is eliminated. The epidermis is used mostly by furriers, though more recent controversies over animal rights have led to a continued decline in the fur trade.

The innermost layer—the subcutaneous, or flesh, later—is where you'll find a line of fat. This is also removed, leaving the dermis. The dermis layer is made up of bundles of fibers and small fibrils, which create a dense mesh. Between all of those fibers are proteins, primarily collagen. Collagen is like the glue of the skin. Its substance makes tanning possible. The denser, upper level of the dermis is the **grain** of the leather, while the lighter underbelly is the split.

Leather manufacturing is made up of three main processes: preparation, tanning, and **crusting**. After that, some leathers receive a surface treatment.

During the first phase of leather preparation, liming, skins are loaded into wooden vats turned and rinsed repeatedly for a full day. Then lime and acids are added to remove any hairs that may still be stuck to the skin. The skins then go back into the wooden vats for another twenty-four-hour cycle of rinsing.

Once the liming is finished, the hides are passed between two rollers. During this fleshing process, one roller is made of rubber and the other is covered in knives, helping to remove the layer of fat and flesh from the dermis.

Next, the leather goes through the splitting process. The skins are put between two rollers, one of which is sharp, splitting the skins evenly throughout. The grain is then ready for tanning.

Tanning is the main process that makes leather, leather. During the tanning process, the leather is pickled and otherwise preserved. There are two main chemical treatments used for leather tanning: chrome and vegetable. **Chrome tanning** results in a light blue colored leather, which can later be blended with a variety of other dyes for coloring.

Vegetable tanning involves treating the hides with various plant extracts. The disadvantage of vegetable tanning is that it doesn't take to dyeing as well. However, leather that has been tanned this way results in an enhanced grain.

Tanned hides are protected from putrification, making them the most widely used for clothing and upholstery nowadays. Rawhide, on the other hand, is still used in very particular circumstances. Anyone who has a dog, for example, probably buys rawhide for the dog to chew on.

The final process of leather making is the crusting process. During these finishing touches, the leather is dried, retanned, thinned, and polished. The first part of crusting is called **sammiering**, where the leather is run through a machine that presses the water out. Then the hides are shaved and trimmed. Then the fresh pieces of leather are chemically dyed based on the manufacturer's needs. The leather then needs to be dried. Next, it is staked, or put in a pinwheel machine for softening.

For a finishing touch, the leather is **buffed**. In the case of **suede**, buffing results in that classic velvety feel. For other leathers, buffing helps correct the grain, removing imperfections like scars, tick bites, or brands. Finally, the leather is sprayed with a finish. Chemicals in the spray make the surface cleanable. They also give leather different finishes—glossy, matte, textured, and more.

Types of Leather

After all of that work, leather comes in four main types: pure **aniline**, semi-aniline, corrected grain, and suede. The purer the leather, the softer it is to the touch. As we know when we go shopping for a leather coat, leather shoes, belts, or cowboy boots, fine leathers are very expensive. As you can see, these objects come from a very complex, long-winded process. These practices are still the basis for leather making in today's market—perhaps one of the oldest inheritances in human history.

ICONIC USES of RAWHIDE and LEATHER

Animal skins have been used as clothing since the beginning of human history. Tarzan and the Flintstones humorously represent leather of the Stone Age in the form of loin cloths and leather ties. During ancient times, Sumerians, Egyptians, and Greeks all used leather as well. Pieces of leather have been found in Egyptian tombs from nearly five thousand years ago. Archaeologists also know that leather strips were used by the Romans to tie togas and piece together armor for their armies.

Two of the more contemporary images of people who wore leather are the gaucho and the vaquero, or what eventually caught on in the American West as the cowboy. The Moors ruled Spain for over seven hundred years. In 1492, Spain rose up, and in turn, colonized others. Upon invading Mexico, Spain's practices of leather braiding expanded when they learned from the Aztecs how to braid rawhide in with the leather. As Spaniards took over haciendas—large estates meant for cattle ranching—leather became a common fabric, especially for men in the field weathering the elements. From boots, to whips, to saddles, leather was a common object. Similar to vaqueros, the gauchos of Argentina were also clad in leather boots. These

Leather was used to make this vaquero's hat, boots, coat, and gauchos.

influences worked their way up to the United States and became part of our image of the cowboy.

While the original image of hides as garments recalls indigenous peoples, cowboys, and utilitarian need in times of survival, by the 1800s, leather also became a marker of high fashion in the United States and Europe.

In 1818, American Seth Boyden began commercial manufacturing of patent leather. Patent leather is coated leather that is very glossy. Boyden began using linseed oil to lacquer the material. These days, most patent leather uses a plastic coating. Accessories with the glass-like look of patent leather usually come in black, though other colors are available during different fashion trends.

Patent leather shoes began being worn by high-society women—a trend that is still in style now. From Salvatore Ferragamo to Manolo Blahnik, the best designers in the world continue to use this product for high-end shoes especially.

Another instant icon comes in the form of the leather jacket. The first leather jackets were brown flight jackets. Aviators and military people wore them. These coats are often called bomber jackets after being worn by aviators during World War II. Many of these coats were made using sheepskin and fleece to offer pilots insulation during extreme climates and elevations. Leather coats shaped like these flight jackets were also worn by Russian Bolsheviks. This uniform was a symbol of Marxism during the Russian Civil War. Likewise, Russia is known for being a cold place, and these coats were made for such elements.

Leather jackets began to infiltrate popular culture during the latter half of the twentieth century, primarily because of their presence in Hollywood. In some cases, Hollywood films depicted World War II. This time in film and TV history also saw *Indiana Jones, Rebel Without a Cause, West Side Story, Grease, Happy Days,* and more.

"Fonzie" or "The Fonz" was known for his laid-back attitude, his enduring loyalty to others, and his leather jacket.

The leather jacket was the emblem of the cool guy on the block. Marlon Brando's character in *The Wild One* rode a motorcycle and was clad in a black leather jacket covered in zippers. Likewise, the Fonz from *Happy Days*, the popular kids in Grease, and the gangs in *West Side Story*, were all identifiably cool and counter to authority by wearing leather jackets. The uniform of young soldiers was now the uniform of a counterculture. To this day, motorcyclists and punk rockers alike wear black leather. From Hollywood to the music industry, the leather jacket is still a sign of cool today.

But the leather jacket is also a sign of high fashion—of the elite. Louis Vuitton, for example, moved from making trunks and durable luggage out of leather to high-end women's purses. Louis Vuitton purses sell today for one to a few thousand dollars a piece. Fine leather is also a luxury product. Pure, soft leathers, like those found along the Mediterranean, are highly sought after. An Italian leather coat can cost thousands of dollars.

LEGACIES

On the one hand, leather is an iconic part of cultural history and Hollywood. On the other hand, leather has been the center of more contemporary fashion controversies. Because leather and fur involve animals, the environmental and political consequences of producing and selling rawhide and leather goods are vaster than most typical textiles.

Leather is a complicated material to make, requiring lots of water, energy, time, and chemicals to make it as luxurious as we demand it should be. Further, the energy used to make leather begins with raising the animal for the hide itself.

Cattle ranching carries with it a great carbon footprint. By breeding cattle for our own purposes, we take up energy, water, and land. The chemical process of tanning also has environmental consequences. The water footprint of making leather is very high—think of the days dedicated to flushing hides with water. Further, the use of chemicals makes the disposal from tanneries dangerous. It also takes leather itself decades to decompose.

Aside from environmental groups, animal rights activists also protest the leather and fur industries. Protests involve phrases like "I would rather go naked than wear fur" and throwing red paint on valuable hide products to symbolize the blood tainting the hands of those who run the industry.

Reigning Style

Leather has become a timeless element in fashion styling and history. From shoes, to handbags, to jackets, leather has proven to keep over long periods of time, making it a marketable investment in high fashion. It might be hard to convince a consumer to spend thousands of dollars on, say, a dress to wear to a wedding—an item of clothing you might only wear once—but a leather coat, on the other hand, can last a lifetime. And it's been consistently in style for men and women for over a century.

All of these processes for leather are seen in our everyday lives. We might not all have a saddle for a horse or a fancy leather coat, but we probably see leather elsewhere. Whether in small accessories like belts, or in furniture, leather still features prominently in our culture.

Leather, despite its contemporary controversy over animal rights, continues to be part of fashion and furniture (especially) because of its strength, durability, and comfort. The technology behind cutting, stripping, and dyeing leather is an old heritage—as old as killing animals for food. And this heritage keeps us comfortable and safe from the elements. Leather couches hold their shape and comfort for decades, as do handbags and coats, all because of the great innovations for manufacturing leather today.

There are few materials as durable as leather. Cotton snags, and nylon runs; most fabrics, in fact, have major weaknesses. On the other hand, leather still is a prevailing image of the rough and tumble West—the cowboy in his boots, his horse saddled. But as textile innovation continued, the effort and energy of killing animals for fabric would be taken over by a new hue of the West: the blue jean.

CHAPTER 3
Blue Jeans

Most of us think of blue jeans as part of an outfit we wear every day. Nowadays, jeans come in many different colors, lengths, and cuts for both women and men. Whether you're a hipster in skinny jeans, a hippie with bell-bottoms, or a worker in carpenter pants, blue jeans are a part of how you express your identity.

Although we think of blue jeans as a common sign of modern times, they have a long history dating back to Italy and France in the sixteenth century and the arrival of a new fabric from **indigo** twill. It would take a lot of time, changing minds, and a number of inventions before blue jeans would be a common fashion item for all.

INVENTIONS that LED to BLUE JEANS

Blue jeans are a landmark of textile history. In order for these trousers to come into being, humans would have to learn a lot about fabric making and dyeing techniques. Blue jeans involve all of the main components of the fashion industry: textiles, design, and merchandising. Some inventions that preceded blue jeans are indigo dye, the cotton gin, buttons, and zippers.

Today, blue jeans are often associated with American culture.

Indigofera Tinctoria

Perhaps the most distinctive quality of blue jeans is that first word: blue. Most fabrics aren't naturally so colorful and alluring—they require dyeing. Though there are many ways to dye something nowadays, the origins of dye come from combining natural products and human ingenuity.

The earliest instances of blue—known in the industry as indigo—are from the flowering plant *Indigofera tinctoria*. The name of this plant indicates the part of the world it hails from: India. During ancient times, the extraction of this color from the plant became part of luxury items for the Greeks and the Romans. Likewise, centuries-old silks and tiling show the use of indigo in many other ancient civilizations: Egypt, Peru, Iran, Africa, and Mesopotamia. India, however, remained the center of indigo dyeing after its origination there.

Indigo would stay luxurious until a synthetic version of the dye came along in the late nineteenth century. In both instances (natural and synthetic), indigo is a challenging dye to use because it requires a precise sequence of dipping the fabric into the dye. After the dyeing process, the fabric is beamed, or wound around a long cylinder, to be collected for transport.

The Cotton Gin

Denim is made out of cotton. It would be impossible to use cotton widely without the cotton gin. Rudimentary versions of the cotton gin have been found from as early as the fifth century CE. In these versions, a roller made out of wood or iron was used to roll out the cotton on a flat surface, like stone or wood. It was a difficult way to separate—or gin out—the seeds from the cotton. But these labor-intensive practices changed in 1794, when Eli Whitney patented the cotton gin.

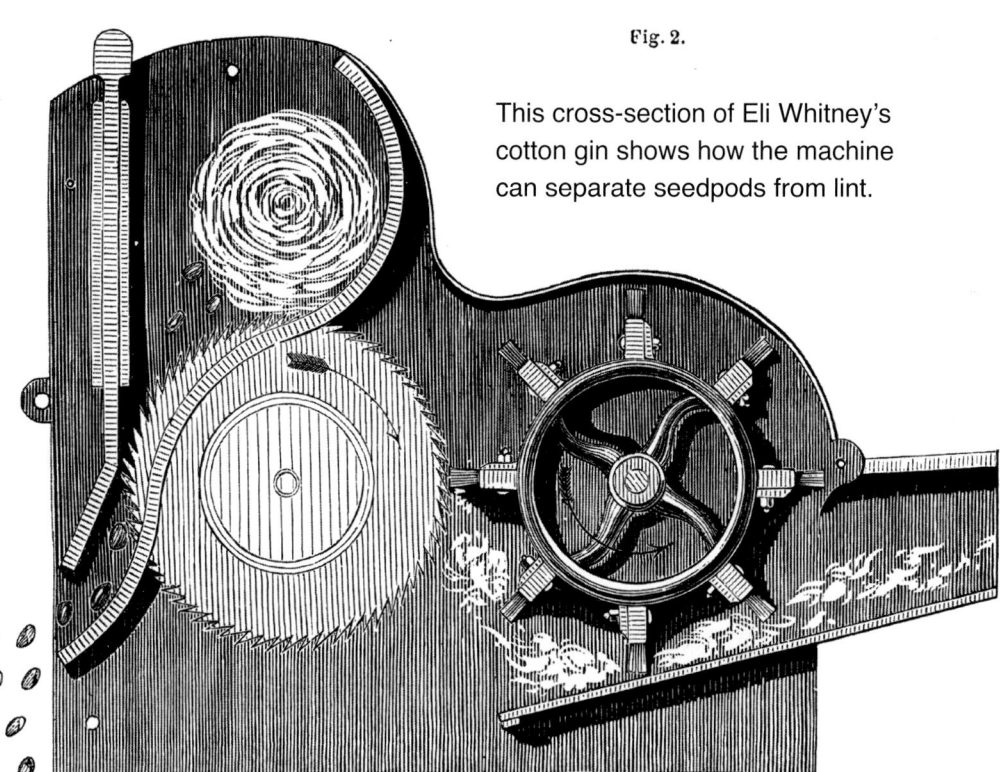

Fig. 2.

This cross-section of Eli Whitney's cotton gin shows how the machine can separate seedpods from lint.

After graduating from Yale University, Whitney moved to Georgia on the invitation of Catherine Greene. Greene and her plantation manager showed Whitney fields of cotton and explained the labor issues behind the high-demand crop. Whitney set out to invent a machine that would quickly and efficiently separate the seedpods, or **bolls**, from the cotton fibers, or **lint**. Unlike models before, Whitney's machine worked like a sieve. A wooden drum embedded with hooks pulled cotton fibers through fine mesh, which collected the bolls with ease. Whitney's original cotton gin was powered by hand cranking. Around 50 pounds (23 kilograms) of cotton could be cleaned in a single day.

Although this invention changed history, it came with consequences. One consequence was that Whitney himself didn't profit much from his idea. He hoped that farmers would rent the gin for periods of time, but they simply stole his idea and made their own versions (though it should be noted that Whitney himself took parts of his idea from Catherine Greene). The biggest consequence was that the cotton gin was, by the mark of many historians, a huge contributing factor to the strengthening of slavery in the American South. With Whitney's invention, growing cotton became an incredibly profitable business. The massive growth in production of cotton meant that plantation owners needed to produce more, faster, meaning an increased demand for land and slave labor.

It seems counterintuitive—the cotton gin was supposed to reduce and lighten the human labor of removing seeds. But because of the cotton boom, more slaves were needed to grow and pick the cotton. Although many Americans were in favor of the abolition of slavery, Congress's incremental ban on slave importation only stopped plantation owners from importing Africans for slave trade but not from trading slaves domestically or keeping slaves' children as slaves.

Buttons

Though we know buttons today as fasteners, the earliest instances of buttons were more for decoration. Found in Pakistan about five thousand years ago, the first buttons fit into loops. By the time of ancient Rome, buttons were used as singular closures for flowing garments, as were broaches and pins. By this time, each of these closures had a practical disadvantage—from poking holes in nice fabrics to being too weak to hold the garment in place.

During the Middle Ages, the button began to change attire entirely. The wealthy used buttons to make more close-fitting clothes. Buttons accentuated the body and created sight lines in clothing. Though this was a sign of the wealthy during the eleventh century, it foreshadowed the commercial and popular use of buttons to come. During the Industrial Revolution, button making became a large-scale manufacturing endeavor. The mass production of buttons led to buttons everywhere—lining shirts, closing shoes, and eventually, closing the top of our favorite trousers: blue jeans.

While new technologies for clothing closure have entered the scene since the rise of the button, the button has remained ever present on our clothes today. Though buttons may take more time to secure than zippers or Velcro, their strength and unassuming presence has kept them in fashion history through the centuries.

Zippers

In 1851, American inventor Elias Howe got a patent for a so-called automatic, continuous clothing closure. Similar to Howe's other huge invention—the sewing machine—he was unable to successfully market his idea. Forty years later, the zipper as we know it would get its chance with inventor Whitcomb Judson. While it would take a few more versions before the zipper became popular and common, these two are responsible for the invention itself. Zippers are still used today for dresses, skirts, shoes, and of course, blue jeans. Without them, we would not have a continuous closure keeping our pants tight.

The INVENTION ITSELF

Blue jeans made their first historic appearance in Genoa, Italy. The Andre family made trousers out of cotton corduroy. This became a common fabric for work clothes in Genoa. In an effort to replicate a sturdy work garment, the French tried to replicate these trousers. In French, "Genoa" is Genes, and these "jeans" were the goal of weavers and seamstresses. In Nimes, France, weavers ended up with a different fabric than the cotton corduroy of Genoa, though. Rather, they had a coarser twill known now as denim, or *de Nimes* ("from Nimes").

Jeans were the defining textile of the working-class in northern Italy in the seventeenth century. In order to accommodate the masses, working clothes were also made out of a cheaper fabric—dungaree—and sold to other countries, such as India and England. Jeans also played a role in the textile trade in utilitarian ways. Genoese sailors would use the textile to cover their goods, proving that the material was made to weather the elements.

While Europe had a glimpse of the original blue jeans, it wasn't until the 1850s that they were introduced in the United States. Blue jeans needed the savvy of American manufacturing and advertising to become not only rampant but iconic.

Levi's

For contemporary people, the history of blue jeans conjures one mythic name: Levi Strauss. Levi's Jeans are still popular to this day; they are sold at Urban Outfitters, stand-alone shops, thrift stores, and department stores. But the history of those jeans, and blue jeans at large, spans an important part of American history.

Levi Strauss was a German Jew born in Bavaria in 1829. He immigrated with his mother and sisters to New York City when he was eighteen. His family had a dry goods business that they expanded across the country over the years. The family decided to open a hub in San Francisco during the California gold rush in 1853, the same year Strauss became an American citizen. Strauss moved to San Francisco to open Levi Strauss & Co., a wholesaler of imported, fine dry goods. He sold everything from clothes, to bedding, to purses, and more.

The gold rush presented new consumers to the market: the western cowboy and miners. Men were heading west in search of fortune. Days quickly turned

Levi Strauss

to months camping out in the wilderness. Men were riding horses, camping, panning in rivers for gold, laying down railroad tracks, and mining. Given the climates and physical demands of the West, sturdier clothes were needed for the journey.

Jacob Davis, a loyal tailor and client of Strauss's, asked Strauss to help him develop clothing reinforced with rivets. Strauss designed the jeans with copper rivets on the pockets. The men received their patent for "improvement in fastening pocket openings" in 1873. These first pants had two pockets in the front and one in the back with copper rivets. The rivets were crucial to the utility of these work pants as they were more likely to hold a tool—like a miner's pick or a wrench—without ripping. Because of their patent number, these jeans are known as the 501s.

Strauss referred to them as "waist overalls." Like bib overalls, jeans were worn loosely. They were primarily utilitarian for the first decades of their existence. They were worn mostly by factory workers, miners, and cowboys. Eventually, the jeans would become iconic. By then, five-pocket jeans became the standard (that fifth, tiny pocket was intended for a pocket watch).

The Production of Blue Jeans

Blue jeans are made today using similar methods to their original manufacture. The advancement of manufacturing technologies has allowed for mass production of these sturdy pants.

The first part of making blue jeans is cotton production. First, cotton must be grown, picked, ginned, and spun into yarn. The yarn is then woven into denim. Denim is noticeable for its diagonal ribbing. This trait results from the **weft**, or the crosswise thread that passes over and under the **warp**, or the vertical threads. In most denim to this day, the warp threads are dyed indigo while the weft thread is kept white.

Dyeing is another crucial element in blue jean production. Denim is dyed—often a blue color, though there are other colors these days too. Originally, natural color dye was used. At the turn to the twentieth century, synthetic indigo was invented and made popular by a German chemist named Adolf von Baeyer. Synthetic dyeing is the most common kind of dyeing when producing blue jeans today.

Denim is then cut and sewn into jeans. An important process introduced by Levi's Jeans in the 1960s is called **pre-shrinking**. These jeans were sized precisely and would not shrink after purchase. This invention led to many later cuts of jeans that the company could sell, such as the 505s (a tighter version of the 501s), the slim boot cut known as the 517s, and even low-rider jeans, which stayed below the waist.

Other modern processes that jeans undergo are distressed looks and sandblasting. Distressed jeans can be acid washed to abrade the fabric. Sandblasting, or abrading with sandpaper, is also used to distress the jeans. These are aesthetic rather than utilitarian processes.

RECEPTION

Blue jeans—from Genoa to America—were well received from the beginning. Jeans became a cultural symbol of workers wherever they were introduced. While we call jeans comfortable, they are, in truth, sturdy and coarse. The story of Levi Strauss's company indicates the rise of America as a world power during the mid-1900s—a country in which new money and new dreams could rise above the rituals of class and old money in worlds past.

LEGACIES

While the miner was the first to wear these jeans for work, the cowboy was the first to ingrain denim into American popular culture. Ever since, American cinema and advertising continue to include denim in their images.

Hollywood

In 1914, American actor William Hart was the first star of popular Western films to be seen clad in blue jeans. A hero in humble attire, Hart was a silent film actor. After World War I, Hollywood blossomed and he grew more and more famous. More popular still was Hollywood actor John Wayne. Wayne and Westerns are synonymous. In 1939, Wayne starred in *Stagecoach* wearing a pair of Levi's 501s.

Singer and actor Bing Crosby took blue jeans into the stratosphere in 1951. He wore all denim to a fancy Canadian hotel and was turned away. Levi Strauss & Co.'s response? They sent him a custom denim tuxedo with a "Notice to All Hotel Men." We still consider denim-on-denim a **Canadian tuxedo** to this day.

The 1950s continued with three of Hollywood's most important stars associating denim with an American aesthetic. Marlon Brando wore 501s (and a leather jacket) in *The Wild One*, a classic motorcycle gang film. James Dean wore them in *Rebel Without a Cause*. Men everywhere began wearing jeans, a white T-shirt, and a leather jacket.

Perhaps most famously, Marilyn Monroe was seen wearing them in *River of No Return* and *The Misfits*. Jeans became a symbol of rebellion.

And as style evolves, Levi Strauss's story continues today. His legacy and fortune are still growing: not only are

Marilyn Monroe famously wore blue jeans in *The Misfits*.

THE LEVI STRAUSS MUSEUM

Levi Strauss was born Loeb Strauss in Buttenheim, Germany, in 1829. Although Strauss's childhood predates World War I and World War II, Jews were already being discriminated against in Bavaria. The government restricted where Jews could live and forced them to pay special taxes, among other discriminatory practices. When Strauss was sixteen, his father died of tuberculosis. Because of his father's death and the increasing discrimination, Strauss made the sojourn to America with his mother and two sisters to meet his older brothers who were already in New York City.

Despite Levi's Jeans' prevalent association with American culture, the same house that Strauss's family was forced to leave in Germany is now the Levi Strauss Museum. In 1983, a woman from Milwaukee, Wisconsin, wrote to the mayor of Buttenheim asking about Levi Strauss's birth and childhood for a German Fest she was hosting. After extensive research, it was finally proven conclusively that Strauss was from Buttenheim indeed. Once the mayor realized Strauss's original home was still standing, the city bought the building and declared it a historical monument.

---

there still Levi's stores and Levi's jeans being sold, there is even the "Field of Jeans"—Levi's Stadium, where the San Francisco 49ers spend their home games each fall.

CHAPTER 4
The Sewing Machine

Just a few hundred years ago, sewing by hand was a skill practiced in every household—a necessary day-to-day skill, not just a hobby as we think of it today. From clothes, to tablecloths, to flags, sails for ships, and wagon covers, every household and many industries relied on stitching. The best in the business were tailors. Today, we may visit a dry cleaner or department

Early sewing factories employed many women and immigrants.

The Sewing Machine 53

store to have our clothes altered to fit. But before the invention of the sewing machine, tailors were used for clothing design, alteration, and general textile needs in a community.

Before the Industrial Revolution, clothes indicated either a fashion sense or a utilitarian need to be dressed. Those who could afford glamorous materials and tailors could afford to focus on fashion. Others wore simple fabrics made of simple shapes that could be sewn by hand at home. The invention of the sewing machine turned clothing manufacturing into a viable large-scale industry, giving rise to a new market altogether.

INVENTIONS that LED to the SEWING MACHINE

Our instant image of sewing is of thread and needle dancing along fabric. These humble objects—needle, thread, fabric—have long relationships with human history. It's hard to imagine a time when man was without clothes, sails for ships, and bedding. Even our earliest images of man involve a loincloth, toga, fishing, and travel by sea. Attaching something to something else is actually a huge feat. And its origins and evolution continue to grow as society evolves, too.

Needles

Sewing dates back as far as twenty thousand years ago. Archaeologists know this from their findings of the earliest needles. From the last Ice Age, archaeologists have found needles that were handmade out of bone. The oldest needles have a split head instead of an eye. Early needles from seventeen thousand years ago have been found in western Europe and central Asia. These large, sharp tools allowed humans to stitch together rawhides and furs for practical uses. Around this time, the first needles with eyes became common. Indigenous Alaskans still use needles to create fur-lined coats and boots to protect from the elements each season presents. Though we think of a needle as a simple object, it went through many transformations to become the modern needle we know today. Even in early history, we see the base material for the needle change from bone, to copper, to bronze, to iron. The next big change in making needles was the use of a **drawing plate**. A drawing plate is a kind of die—a special tool used to cut and shape materials. The drawing plate is made of a hardened steel plate across which there are many holes of different diameters. Wire is *drawn* through a hole to make it thinner. This process can be done by hand and was used in making steel needles.

The INVENTION ITSELF

The sewing machine was one of many inventions in the mid-1800s that profoundly changed human life. Not only did a whole new industry open up employment, trade, distribution, and commercial sales opportunities, but it also alleviated women in every household from the time-consuming and daunting task of sewing by hand.

Early Versions of the Sewing Machine

The history of the sewing machine is not as simple as Isaac Singer's invention, though that might be the first image of a sewing machine that springs to mind. As historians argue and work to keep the history of the sewing machine alive and well, there are a few names that always come up in the conversation of this machine's narrative.

First is Charles Fredrick Wiesenthal. Wiesenthal was born in Germany and was living in London in 1755 when he applied for a patent that would change sewing forever. Wiesenthal's needle was double-pointed, with an eye on one end meant for mechanical use. Though he hadn't drawn out plans for the machine that could host the needle, many feel his contribution and needle patent mark the beginning of the sewing machine.

In 1790, the first sewing machine was invented by Thomas Saint of England. Saint was a cabinetmaker. His vision of the sewing machine was primarily to join leather and canvas together to produce more durable boots, saddles, bridles, and more. Saint's machine had an awl that first pierced a hole in the leather and then passed a needle and thread through it, forming a **chain stitch**. Other features of Saint's machine included a looper, an overhanging arm, and a feed mechanism—many recognizable features of sewing machines today.

But Saint's idea was not supported by a working model—it was only a patent for an idea. It's likely he tried building a model, but nothing was ever found. He overlooked Wiesenthal's double-pointed needle, which could have helped his invention get off the ground. He was not able to successfully advertise his idea either. And so Saint's drawings remained as drawings.

Shortly thereafter, the race to the first sewing machine was on. An Austrian tailor, Josef Madersperger, received a patent for a working machine in 1814 after working on many versions. He spent the next two decades trying to make the machine work smoothly, receiving grants from the government, but none the elements came together to make one working machine, no matter how many drafts he tried.

Simultaneously, Thomas Stone and James Henderson were working in France on their own version of a sewing machine made to replace hand sewing. Likewise, a man named Scott Duncan began working on a multiple-needle machine for embroidery.

In 1818, America saw its first claim in the race when John Adams Doge and John Knowles invented a working device. Though it could make a stitch, the machine could only handle a small piece of material before needing to be reset entirely, and thus, it wasn't practical.

In 1829, the sewing machine would become practical. French tailor Barthélemy Thimonnier wanted to build a machine that would make his vocation easier, faster, consistent, and even more expert. His machine was made almost entirely of wood. He used a barbed needle for the machine that produced a chain stitch (as idealized by Saint). Thimonnier was granted the patent for the first sewing machine in 1830.

Unlike Saint, Thimonnier convinced those in power that a sewing machine was useful. Thimonnier received a contract to build a set of machines meant for making army uniforms. He opened the first machine-based clothing manufacturer in the world less than ten years after receiving his patent. Thimonnier's success makes him the first big name still associated with the invention of this world-changing machine today.

Back in America, the first **lockstitch** sewing machine was invented by Walter Hunt in 1832. Hunt's machine used an **eye-pointed needle**, in which an eye and point are on the same end of the needle. The needle itself was curved and moved through fabric horizontally. Like many other attempts, Hunt's machine suffered from an inadequate feed for the fabric. He didn't even patent his version in the end.

John Greenough used Hunt's eye-pointed needle to patent the first American sewing machine in 1842. Greenough introduced two pressing surfaces to hold the fabric in position while the eye-pointed needle was at work. While this was a good revision of Hunt's work, missing elements prevented the machine from becoming popular.

In 1844, Elias Howe created a sewing machine that held the fabric vertically and received a patent for it. This

This wood engraving of Isaac Singer's first sewing machine shows many important features still used today, like the puller feed, needle feed, and rotating hook.

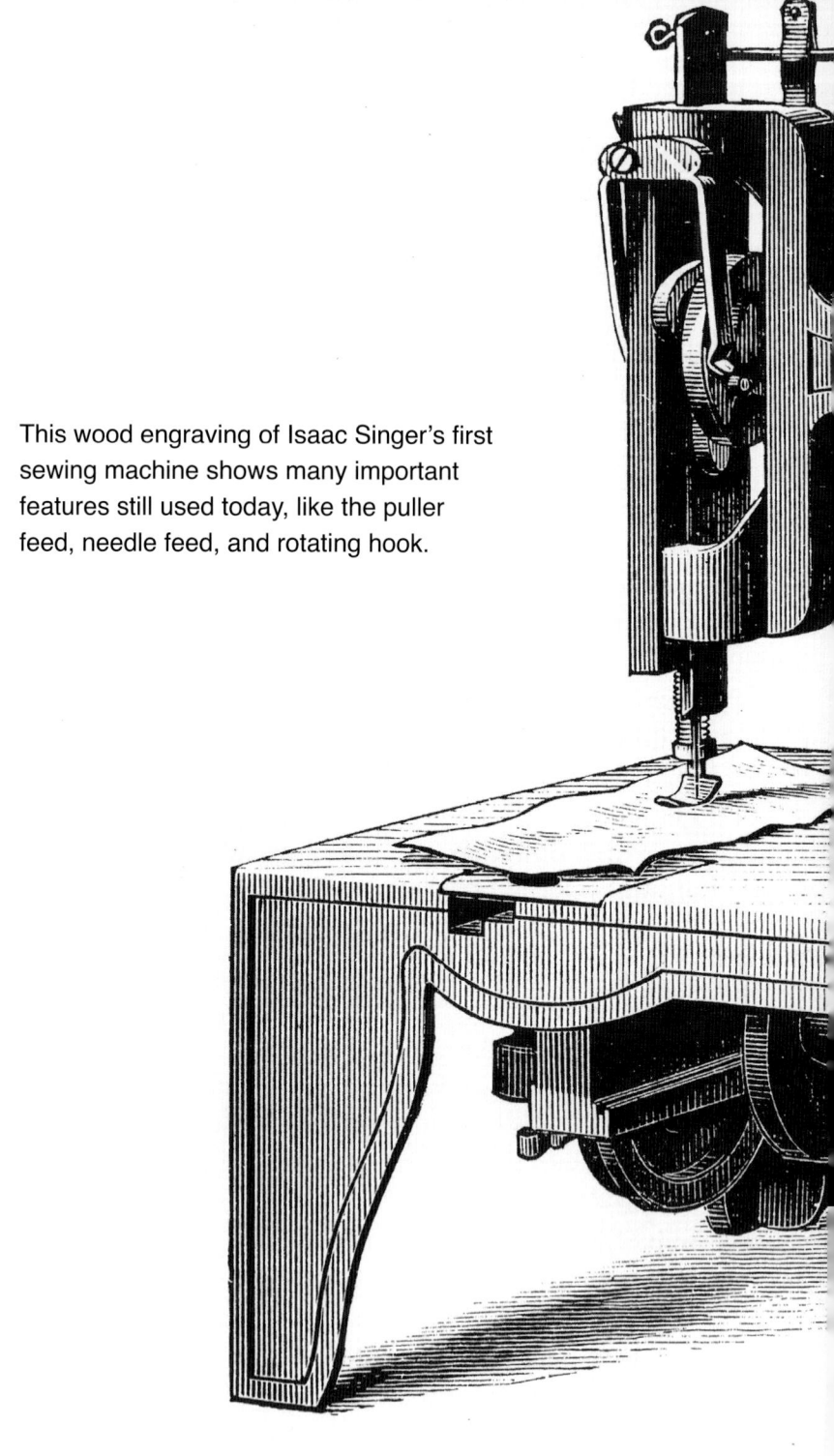

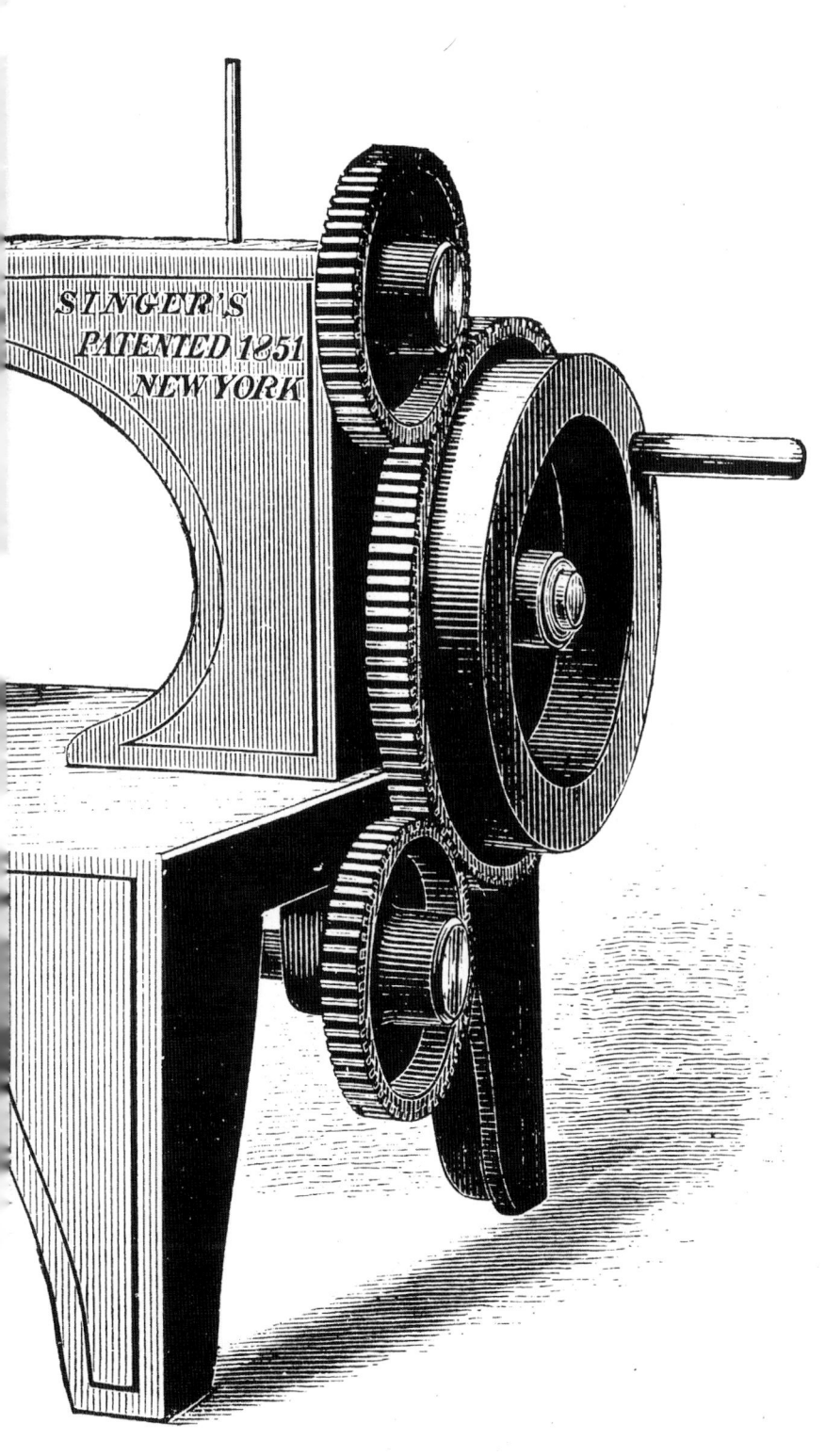

lockstitch machine had an eye-pointed needle, a shuttle beneath the fabric to form the lockstitch, and an automatic feed. Though it could out-stitch any human, he was unable to sell the machine. Howe went to England to try to garner interest. Yet the sewing machine wouldn't take off until Isaac Singer led the way in America.

Though the machines and ideas of these tailors and inventors seem like failures, they fed into the larger success of a working sewing machine. Each one represents a phase of the scientific method. Where one man was unable to successfully pierce the material, another was able to feed fabric into the machine, and so on. Each mistake inspired a new idea toward a correction, finally leading to the sewing machine as we know it today.

"The Queen of Inventions"

Isaac Singer. His name is still the biggest one in sewing machines today. While others had tried to make a working sewing machine, Singer was the first to make a practical one, combining all the elements of sewing machines prior.

Singer was an artist. Not a designer, tailor, or painter as we might guess, but rather, an actor. While his career was slow to get off the ground, he had invented a machine that could drill into rock. He sold it for $2,000. With a bit of money in his pocket, he tried to return to acting. As that life continued to present hardships to his career and to his family—eight children and his wife—Singer went back to the drawing board.

Next he developed a woodblock cutting machine. After many failed attempts and a steam-boiler explosion, Singer and his family moved from New York City to Boston for a new start. As he continued to work on new machines for print presses, mechanics sought his advice on how to make a working sewing machine.

Singer realized that while stiches create a loop, the machine's motion did not need to mimic that circular

Isaac Singer

motion. Singer was the first to suggest and make a machine that abandoned the curved needle for a straight one and moved the shuttle in a straight motion instead of a circular one.

Singer worked for eleven days and eleven nights building his own sewing machine incorporating these ideas. His version was powered by a treadle—a foot petal. At first, when he tried stitching, the thread bunched into loops. Going back through the scientific method, Singer hypothesized that if the thread were more taut, it wouldn't bunch up. His son pulled a spring out of his toy popgun for his father. Singer added the spring to the machine, allowing it to make smooth, tight stitches. Singer's machine could sew nine hundred stitches per minute. The most expert seamstress at the time would only have been able to make about forty per minute.

With his newfound invention, Singer saw an opportunity for profit. He placed an advertisement in the newspaper that simply said "SEWING BY MACHINERY." Crowds gathered to see the machine. Seamstresses and tailors faced off to try to beat the machine, but none could match its nearly one thousand stitches per minute. The impression the machine left on the community earned it the title "Queen of Inventions," as coined by a magazine.

RECEPTION

Like many inventions during the Industrial Revolution, the sewing machine stood to change everything. Singer saw this object as an opportunity not just to make money but to expand the use of machines in daily lives.

To be sure, Singer was a businessman as much as he was an inventor. His ingenuity was not reserved solely for machines but also for the savvy ways he was able to get this big, new machine out to the public.

THE TAILORS' UPRISING

Inventions cause change. And when people's lives stand to change by the hands of others, they can become fearful. In France, when tailors found out about Thimonnier's sewing machines, they feared that their profession would become obsolete. Late one night, a group of tailors stormed Thimonnier's machine shop. They destroyed every machine.

Thimonnier and a business partner were able to make another machine with some improvements, but the Parisian tailors stormed his factory again and burned it to the ground. France was on the brink of a revolution. Thimonnier took the parts of one salvageable machine and fled for England. Despite the fact that he was the first inventor of the machine, the first to sell machines commercially, and the first to develop and run a garment factory, Thimonnier died a poor man in 1857.

Today, we are awed by new inventions, but many remain concerned that new inventions might replace human skills. Machines and technology threaten jobs all the time. As we adapt to these new machines, new kinds of jobs develop around them. The fashion industry sees these exciting and terrifying changes all the time.

Production, Sales, and Cost

In America, Singer's machine impressed the masses. With a new, high demand, Singer set out to give the people what they wanted. At first, sewing machines were too expensive. Singer had a workshop where each machine was made by hand and fitted together. In order to get rich, Singer needed to make a machine that everyone could afford. Similar to the way a scientist uses the scientific method, Singer applied those ideas to business. Instead of making each machine by hand, he'd figure out how to make every part of the machine exactly alike to put them together quickly.

While Singer began this version of making the machines, he needed more money. He decided to let people pay five dollars up front to bring the machine home and let them pay the rest of the cost over time—today, this is known as the hire-purchase system. People would save for their five-dollar down payment, and pay the rest in installments each month until they'd purchased the machine in full.

Another insight Singer had related to teaching. Singer sent salesmen to customers' homes to teach them how to use this new, fancy machine. They taught customers all over the country how to adjust, oil, and stitch using their new machine. Men could carry the machines on their backs to a factory where they made clothes, out-stitching tailors of the old world. Fashion began changing, too. More complicated designs, such as elaborate dress ruffles, showed off the skills of using a sewing machine.

Consumerism began to change as more could be produced quickly. From caps, to overcoats, to boots, suitcases, uniforms, purses, and theater curtains, everyday objects required far less power and time than they once had. Garment factories became rampant by 1870. Rooms full of hundreds of sewing machines produced thousands of garments. Mail-order catalogues came into being, allowing people to buy clothing from anywhere in the country.

As the machines became more and more popular, so did the competition. Instead of letting others outdo him, Singer purchased others' creative patents and used the ideas to improve upon his machine. The treadle eventually disappeared when the machine could be electrically powered. And instead of buying a new machine, people could trade out their old machine from their initial down payment for a new one.

LEGACIES

A whole way of life changed because of Singer's machine. Women and girls were the primary sewers in each household. Either by saving time using a sewing machine to make clothes or being able to affordably buy clothes, women suddenly had substantially more time on their hands. Many used their skills to become employed by garment factories. Others were able to go to school—a privilege women were not given before.

Every household to this day is impacted by the sewing machine—from rugs, to furniture, to suitcases, to clothing and shoes, many objects we encounter owe a lot to this machine. Further, the hire-purchase system, the change in consumer habits, and the industrial model owe a great deal to Isaac Singer.

CHAPTER 5
Rayon

Rayon is a textile fabric. Unlike many textiles that come to mind first—cotton, wool, silk, linen—rayon is not a natural fiber. Rayon is the first artificial fabric used in clothes. Rayon stands for change—in fashion, history, and cultural ideals. While it's use changed many practical things in fashion, the simple fact that *any* artificial fabric is possible represents a big shift in industrialization.

Rayon's history involves as much promise and excitement as it does terror and despair. Though it is only a humble fabric, its ability to seem like other fabrics made it powerful, nearly magical. Women who couldn't afford silk could suddenly wear something that looked an awful lot like it. Manufacturers who were short on cotton production suddenly didn't need to rely on nature to grow enough. Instead, they could fabricate it in a lab. Rayon is a feat of chemistry. Its introduction to the market marks the beginning of a technological and digital era of the fashion industry. On the other hand, synthetic fabrics cost thousands of people their jobs. With the advent of rayon, textile manufacturing would ever be the same.

Today, we can find rolls and rolls of thread and textiles at our local craft and fabric stores.

ACETYLATION: The PROCESS That LED to RAYON

Though we needed a tremendous amount of discovery in chemistry to bring the image of invented fabric to the world, the attempts began long before rayon was finally invented.

Fibers that are made from natural products are known in chemistry as cellulosic. In 1865, Paul Shützenberger and Laurent Naudin produced the first cellulose acetate through a process called acetylation, which involves treating cellulose with acid compounds.

In 1910, Camille and Henry Dreyfus were using acetate to develop motion picture film. As they used acetate yarn, these brothers began to see its other potential

Camille Dreyfus

applications. Perfecting acetate plastic and lacquers led them to helping the United States government work on American warplanes for World War I. By 1924, the government had asked them to set up a factory in Maryland. Camille paved the way in business and branding of this new yarn, turning it into a commercial fabric. What had been referred to as "imitation silk" for nearly forty years finally had a name of its own as given by the Federal Trade Commission (FTC): rayon.

Without initial experiments with acetylation, many of the chemical developments necessary to pave the way to rayon (in its many forms) wouldn't be possible. As with all scientific discoveries, the scientific method allowed these chemists to test hypotheses until finding a resolution. In conjunction with Camille's business savvy, rayon would be able to change the world as we know it.

The INVENTION ITSELF

Rayon is a result of generating cellulose and combining it with acids to make something chemically novel. Chemistry is potion making in real life—a seemingly magical and complex practice. It's hard to understand how these atoms can change properties without a microscope and a lot of knowledge. Yet the result of such "magic" is a fabric that is multi-faceted and chameleon like.

Rayon can be made out of different chemical elements. It can be turned into multiple imitations of fabric. Whether mimicking the softness of silk, the functionality of cotton, or standing on its own as nylon, rayon is a master of disguise.

Rayon's Evolution

The first patent for an artificial fiber went to a Swiss chemist, Georges Audemars, in 1855. Audemars successfully dissolved the inner bark of a mulberry tree and chemically changed it to make cellulose. Audemars's version of fiber production was highly time consuming and inefficient. Although Audemars's fiber was not commercially viable, he discovered and invented the first artificial fabric—what he referred to as artificial silk.

A few decades later, chemist and electrician Sir Joseph Swan entered the scene. One important change from the time of Audemars's initial patent is that Thomas Edison had invented the incandescent lightbulb by Swan's era. Taking a note from Edison, Swan used Audemars's solution but put it through fine holes in a coagulating bath. Swan's new process had applications to electricity, and so his work made its way back to Edison. Swan knew it could be used for textiles too, though. Swan gave the fibers to his wife and had her crochet some fabric. In 1885, he showed her work at an exhibit in London to inspire other textile applications stemming from his process and ideas.

The year 1885 also proved a turning point for one French chemist, Count Hilaire de Chardonnet. During the 1860s, the silk industry was in crisis. French silkworms were diseased, and production was at a standstill. Chardonnet and Louis Pasteur worked together to try to solve the problem. During their collaboration, Chardonnet realized that, though it wouldn't save the silkworms, making an artificial silk could save the industry. His patent for the process of making artificial fiber was granted in 1885. In 1889, artificial silk finally debuted and became a full-blown sensation. Chardonnet was the first to produce artificial silk—rayon—at a commercial scale. He first exhibited his version at a Paris exhibition. Unlike the other inventors, Chardonnet was business minded enough to build the first plant for production of "Chardonnet silk." His efforts brought him to fame as "father of the rayon industry." Those who followed him created more cost-effective ways of making rayon, but the title remained all Chardonnet's.

By the early 1900s, the Dreyfus brothers were making headway. In fact, the Dreyfus brothers were ahead of other chemists because they had worked with acetylation. Camille was able to beat everyone else and become the first man to establish a business using rayon as a textile. By the mid-1920s, everything about textiles and the world was changing, and rayon was at the center of it all.

The Mechanics of Rayon

Man-made fibers can be categorized in two ways: natural (made of cellulosic fibers) or synthetic (made of noncellulosic polymer fibers). Although rayon is artificial, its origins are natural. The natural base from which rayon is made is cellulose, a substance that comes from plant and vegetable cell walls. It is characterized by very technical chemical properties that chemists and biologists study to understand how plants break down. Cellulose's highest natural concentration is in wood pulp—pine, spruce,

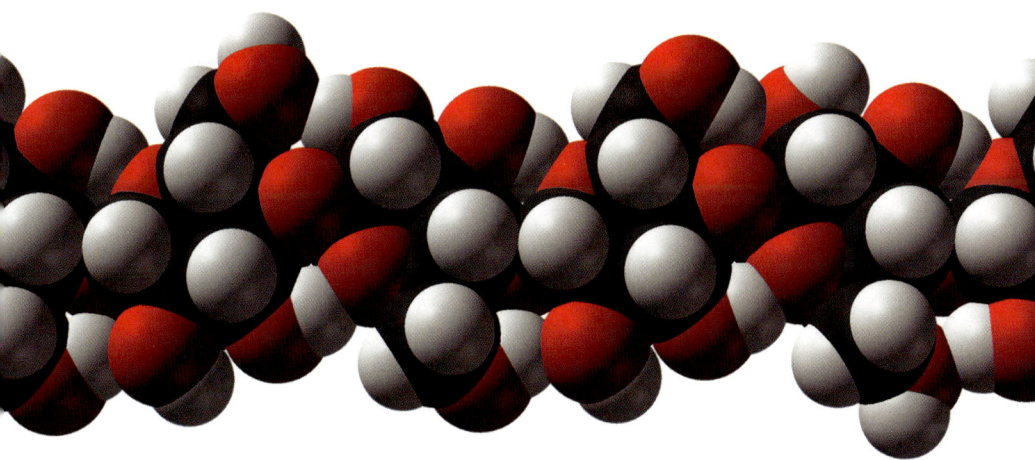

This is a big-picture look at the crystal structures of cellulose, which account for the thread's flexibility.

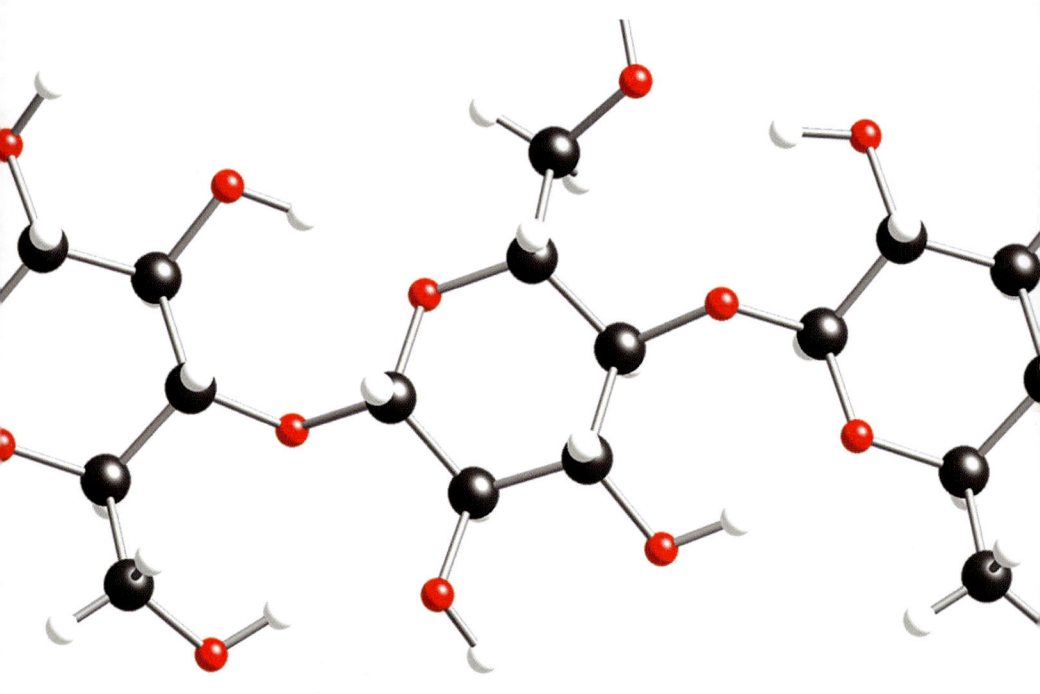

This ball-and-stick model of cellulose shows the positions of atoms and the bonds between them.

hemlock. It's also found in cotton linters (residue that sticks to the bolls after being ginned).

There are two main types of rayon: viscose rayon and high-wet-modulus (HWM) rayon. In both cases, the natural origin—cellulose—is changed chemically and regenerated (the mark of a synthetic fiber). Extracted and purified cellulose becomes a white cellulose sheet. The cellulose sheet is then steeped in caustic soda, resulting in alkali cellulose. Once the sheets dry, they are crumbled. The crumbles are placed in a metal container for two to three days. Then, the crumbs are combined and churned with another liquid chemical—carbon disulfide. The result of that process is regenerated, orange cellulose. It's dipped again in caustic soda, where it turns into a syrupy version

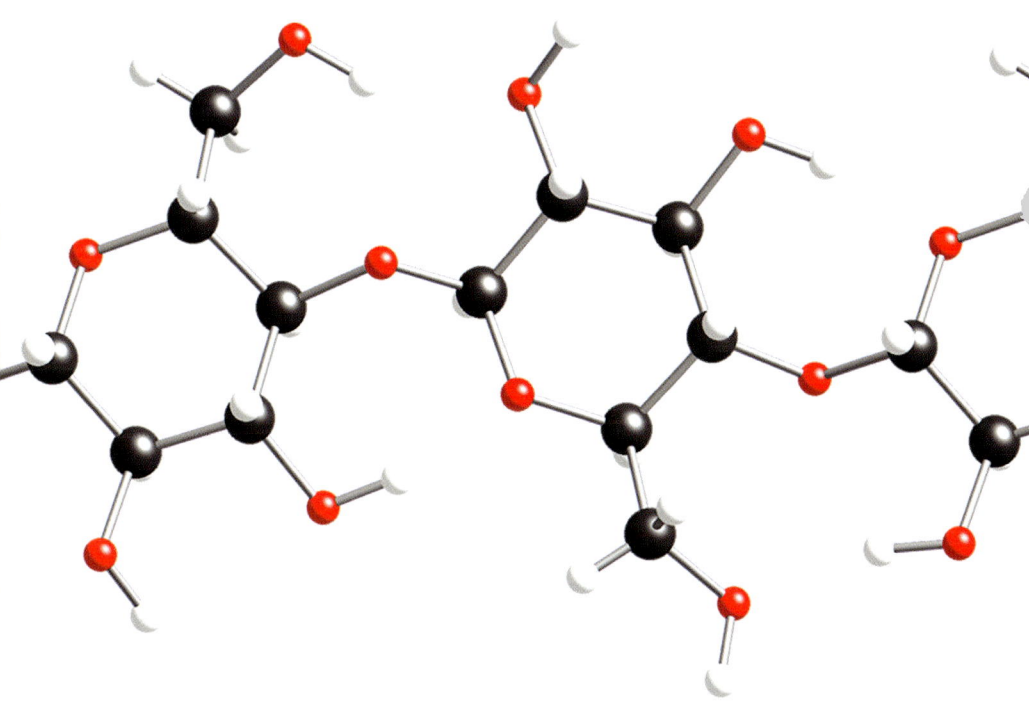

of itself. After another few days, this "syrup" becomes rayon **filaments**.

Just as rayon was made, in part, to resolve the looming silk crisis, making rayon is similar to silk manufacturing. With silk, silkworms transform the cellulose of, say, a mulberry tree into two fine filaments. With cellulose rayon, a liquid version of cellulose is forced through a nozzle. This spinneret is perforated like a showerhead. A filament comes through each hole and is then dipped into an acid bath, where it firms up. These filaments are twisted to make rayon yarn.

Another incarnation of rayon is called high-wet-modulus rayon. As the rayon industry continued to grow, scientists began making the fabric stronger. Viscose rayon had limitations. Primarily, it can lose most of its strength when wet. In 1952, the term "wash and wear" was coined to describe a new cotton blend to the public, and so rayon needed to rise to the occasion.

Manufacturers started producing HWM rayon to stay relevant in the textile revolution.

When processing HWM rayon, only slight adjustments are made to the cellulose rayon production process: Filaments are stretched longer. A weaker caustic soda is used. And no aging is involved in any part of the process.

RECEPTION

Rayon could and can be produced quickly and at a low cost. The advantage of these kinds of materials stood (and still stand) to change the market. On the one hand, these low-cost, low-energy products are to be championed in capitalism; these objects give the masses access to the same product. However, the demand for rayon in conjunction with time when it entered the American market symbolizes the more complex economic issues of textiles.

Decline of American Textile Industry

In the late 1920s, America experienced its largest economic crisis to date, marking the period known as the Great Depression. Rayon contributed to the decline of America's textile industry. Wool, cotton, and silk stood no chance next to rayon. They were highly expensive comparatively, with rayon costing about half the amount of silk.

While the other fabrics had their history, heritage, and industry around them, rayon's ability to blend with other fabrics and become whatever the weaver chose left consumers in an already terrible economic situation with no choice: rayon was the affordable material.

Although rayon was initially meant for men's business socks, it quickly became common to see women's lingerie made from the fabric. Rayon then gave way to nylon, and a whole world of advertising and fashion was reborn. While all of this seems like a change for the better, there were consequences for those employed in textile manufacturing. Rayon's rise made it difficult for other textile companies to stay in business, let alone keep employees.

LEGACIES

After forty years of "imitation silk," the FTC finally recognized the novelty and potential of rayon and gave it a worthy name. Initially, "rayon" was meant to describe any man-made fiber made from cellulose. As chemistry around cellulose and acetylation progressed, the FTC changed their method of classifying rayon. In 1952, rayon was divided into two categories: pure cellulose (rayon), and those consisting of a cellulose compound (acetate).

Rayon is still widely used today. Like many contemporary textiles, though, its existence is shaped by world markets. Historically, rayon's effect on these markets has played an important role, too. Rayon has other, more surprising legacies as well. The fabric fundamentally altered the cotton industry and has profound environmental consequences.

Replacing Cotton

Around 2010, the price of cotton was so high that many clothing manufacturers replaced it with rayon in their fabrics and fabric blends. This increased demand for rayon has its own consequences, though. For one thing, pulp mills are getting a second life. Companies are investing in these facilities to quickly turn wood pulp into fiber boards or threads. Also, because of the increased demand, rayon is more expensive these days than it was originally. It still has a price advantage over cotton, but perhaps not for long.

During the Great Depression, many factories closed, leaving people jobless and penniless.

Environmental Impact

The energy used to make and distribute textiles is vast and complicated. In the case of rayon, much of the environmental controversy comes from production itself. Although HWM rayon seems easier to make and manage, it requires lignin-free cellulose as its starting point. Viscose rayon is much cheaper because it requires wood as its source of cellulose.

Because of this economic factor, many factories choose to use viscose rayon in their clothes and other products. The viscose process, unfortunately, produces huge amounts of contaminated waste. This waste in the water and the air is devastating to the natural world. The chemicals and acidity of such wastewater stand to destroy animal life, ecosystems, and the sea.

The more water-repellent the rayon-based fabric is (such as HWM rayon), the longer it takes to biodegrade. It does biodegrade faster than cotton, but that's not saying much. Many marine creatures eat rayon fibers that are dumped into the sea. It can be fatal if it ends up in their bloodstream. Rayon makes up about 57 percent of fibers found in the deep ocean. Many manufacturers are trying to reduce pollution. Hopefully, someone will come up with a resolution before too much damage is done.

Rayon's Future

Despite rayon's current environmental impact, rayon is still a prominent textile in today's world. In fact, the demand for rayon is higher than ever. New technologies will continue to make rayon better and cheaper.

Another notable trend that has affected rayon is the cultural fluctuation between natural materials and synthetic materials. Although the introduction of rayon disrupted the natural material market, natural fabrics have experienced a

GORE-TEX

Rayon is not our only synthetic, flexible fabric. One many of us encounter every day is Gore-Tex. Gore-Tex is a flexible, breathable fabric, but more usefully, it's waterproof. We might find it in our clothes or gear for skiing, hiking, aqua sports, and the like.

Like many feats of scientific genius, Gore-Tex was a happy accident in 1969. The Gore brothers—Wilbert and Robert—were working with a material called Teflon. Teflon has many uses that we still see today. Teflon is the coating that makes our pans "non-stick." Teflon is so strong and nonreactive that it's also commonly found in surgical materials because bacteria can't eat away at it or stick to it.

The Gore brothers were heating long rods of Teflon in order to find out if they could stretch it. In their impatience, they yanked the rod instead of stretching it slowly. To their surprise, Teflon stretched and stretched and stretched. This stretched version is their patented gold, Gore-Tex. By stretching the Teflon, a lot more air enters the material making it highly lightweight while keeping the resistant properties of Teflon. After a battle with another inventor who was secretly making Teflon tape, the Gore brothers kept their patents. Gore-Tex is still used widely by manufacturers like the North Face, Patagonia, Marmot, L.L. Bean, and pretty much any other outdoor lifestyle brand you could think of. From tents to gloves, adventuring is perhaps less comfortable and dry without Gore-Tex.

---

resurgence. In the 1970s, synthetic polyester was everywhere. But over time, consumers resented that it didn't "breathe" the way natural fabrics did. Now the trend is blended fabrics, which combine naturals and synthetics, and rayon often serves as the synthetic element of a blend. Rayon's chemical makeup allows it to blend well with others.

Likewise, rayon is perhaps poised to change the landscape of chemistry once again. Scientists seem to be on the brink of producing cellulose from sunlight, water, or carbon dioxide. This could be hugely cost effective and much safer for the environment. Rayon's endless flexibility keeps it alive and relevant as the decades go by.

The Rise of Synthetic Fabrics

Another notable legacy of rayon is that it paved the way for all kinds of inventions in textiles. Chemists were able to enter the fashion world and bring their highly technical and scientific findings into everyday use. After cellulose acetate, chemists began experimenting with changing the natural makeup of materials. Synthetic fabrics look more like plastic than plants when looked at with a microscope. We use them today in the form of elastic, rayon, nylon, spandex, Kevlar, and many more.

SPANDEX/LYCRA

Spandex is a synthetic material found in the majority of closets. Spandex is found in athletic apparel, swimwear, volleyball shorts, dance clothes, socks, tights, leggings, ski pants, wetsuits, underwear, belts, bra straps, and even skinny jeans. Spandex is more durable than natural rubber.

This strength and durability is by design. Joseph Shivers was a chemist for DuPont's Virginia laboratory. He was brought on to find a synthetic way to replace rubber. He discovered spandex in 1958. Spandex expands, and so its name is an anagram of "expands." Shivers was dead set on perfecting a new polyester (another synthetic) with his findings. By 1959, spandex was renamed Lycra and was ready to be presented to the public. (While many countries still call it Lycra, it's referred to more commonly as spandex in the United States.)

Spandex, like rayon and Gore-Tex, is made through the scientific method, requiring many precise steps. The right chemicals need to be mixed—or reacted—in order to change their properties and make them something else. The precise chain reaction then needs to be spun into spandex fibers. Without chemists, all of that reacting, melting, and spinning would be impossible, and we would not have synthetic fabrics or coatings, which have all kinds of uses in our everyday lives.

While we might not be wearing volleyball spandex or a wetsuit every day, since being invented, spandex is blended into about 80 percent of clothing sold in the United States alone. It's often mixed with cotton or other fabrics to give people the same feel as natural fibers yet make them more durable.

A runway model shows off a dress crafted from 3D-printed panels.

CHAPTER 6
The Future of Fashion

"In a machine age, dressmaking is one of the last refuges of the human, the personal, the inimitable."
—Christian Dior

Fashion has grown by leaps and bounds since the days of bone needles and handlooms. While we once spent time making and repairing our own clothes, we now spend it out shopping. Now, alongside Hollywood and advertising, social media has also entered the scene and changed what it means to be a fashion icon.

TECHNOLOGY and FASHION

The invention of the internet changed every aspect of human life. Thanks to the internet, clothing companies, department stores, and new fashion companies are able to sell their products with the click of a button. And while many stores did not adapt to this shift and had to close their doors, those who did evolve have benefitted from increased sales made online.

Shopping is not the only aspect of the fashion world that has changed because of technology. Our digital era has had fashion magazines, design software, merchandising, and more move to the online sphere. Here are a few technologies that are changing the way the art of fashion is practiced.

Digital Textile Printing

Fabric painting has been around for centuries. Early practices of fabric printing involved block or relief printing, in which dye is pressed onto fabric from a carved block. In this old way of printing, the dye is applied to the surface of the fabric.

By the eighteenth century, printers had advanced this method to use rollers to move fabric under the block. This process made multiple-color and faster printing possible. During the twentieth century, screen printing became the most common practice of textile printing. A roller is used to ink a stencil that applies a design on the fabric.

Now, computers allow us to print on textiles as we would print out a piece of paper from a computer. Ink-jet printing is used for printing T-shirts and other promotional wear. Printing designs onto larger textile rolls is becoming increasingly popular, especially for promotional goods and advertising. Companies can print their logo or message easily on flags, banners, and fabric signs.

Fashion Design and Styling Software

Since the rise of laptop computers, fashion design has gone digital. Even designers who prefer to draw by hand have the option of doing so digitally using tablets and touch-screen laptops. Today there are even digital notebooks that transfer hand drawings to software instantly. Perhaps the savviest digital notebook so far is the Livescribe Notebook by Moleskine. Using a special Livescribe smartpen, whatever you write or draw in your Moleskine notebook appears on your computer, smartphone, or tablet.

Livescribe Notebooks allow users to draw and write on both real and virtual surfaces.

Design software also comes in many incarnations for fashion designers and stylists. Whether you're a commercial designer, an amateur, or a high-fashion designer, there's a program for you. There are programs dedicated to designing and printing clothing labels. There are programs for calculating accurate measurements for pattern making. Of course, there is also an array of programs you can use to make professional clothing designs.

3D Printing

The meaning of the word "designer" has expanded to include engineers. Similar to the tailors of the past who rallied against Thimonnier's machine, fashion designers who grew up drawing and sewing are being replaced by those who can use technology in their design processes.

Software is just one way that designers' skills have transformed. But successful new artists in fashion need to be forward thinking. Just like Chanel, who was able to use fashion to reflect the changed and changing world for women, fashion designers today are successful when they embrace technology.

Fashion trends have been influenced by technological advancements for some time. Aerospace and automobile design features and technology impact aspects of trends like shapes, colors, and materials. At the forefront of design technology is 3D printing. With a 3D printer, a three-dimensional object can be printed from a digital file. The potential applications are vast: from printing human organs to architectural models, every part of the human experience stands to benefit from this invention.

The 3D printer stands to be as revolutionary as the sewing machine. Software engineers can design algorithms for dress printing. Tough fabrics like nylon are suddenly flexible when imprinted with interlocking patterns meant to mimic knitting or crocheting. The result, so far, has been garments and accessories created in a futuristic style. The 3D printer has changed our understanding of what garments are, how they should fit, how much they should cost, and what they say about our digital world.

These exciting and groundbreaking ideas were shown at the 2016 Met Gala, "Manus x Machina: Fashion in an Age of Technology." One piece worn featured in this costume ball was a crystal dress with movable pieces controlled by a remote. As 3D printers become more affordable and powerful, we may eventually live in a world where we print our own clothes in the morning to reflect our mood.

The Met Museum's "Manus × Machina" exhibit featured nearly two hundred pieces of clothing.

CONTEMPORARY CONTROVERSIES

Technological advancement is just one change in the fashion industry. And change often breeds controversy. As fashion houses and retailers continue to produce a staggering amount of clothes each year, ethical dilemmas arise. Controversies in fashion can be found at nearly every turn. The main issues facing the industry are appropriation of goods and styles, environmental consequences, and illegal labor practices.

Appropriation

Appropriation of style is a common problem in our clothes. Appropriation is the action of taking something for your own use without an owner's permission. In the arts, this can be the stealing of ideas, techniques, patterns, and more.

Major retailer Urban Outfitters is no stranger to controversies involving appropriation. At the level of fashion design, they are notorious for stealing artists' work and selling it in their stores without acknowledging or compensating artists. They have been known to send corporate and marketing staff to scout new trends in fashion. When they find an artisan's work they like, they develop a similar product. Everything from jewelry to geo-printed skirts has been found at Urban Outfitters. Sometimes, people make a loud enough noise about it on social media and the piece is pulled, usually labeled "sold out" on the UO website.

Yet UO is not the only retailer guilty of appropriation. Corporations make millions of dollars marketing "tribal prints," for instance. These companies do not compensate the indigenous cultures responsible for these designs.

Environment

When we think of pollution, we often think of smokestacks, mining towns, oil rigs, and clogged sewers leading to water, not the little black dress. However, fashion is the world's second biggest pollutant, following behind the oil industry.

As we've seen with rawhide, the sewing machine, blue jeans, and rayon, complex processes are behind the clothes sold in stores. The business of fashion includes textile manufacturing, raw material production, clothing construction, shipping, and retail. This does not even account for our use of the clothes, which involves multiple washes and (eventually) the disposal of garments.

The cumulative result of these processes is pollution. The carbon footprint of each garment we purchase is high.

The natural resources that are extracted in order to go through all of those supply chains is another element of fashion's steep environmental cost.

Even humble cotton, that seemingly natural and simple fabric, still causes a lot of damage. It takes nearly 5,000 gallons (19,000 liters) of water to grow and manufacture the materials to make just one T-shirt and one pair of jeans!

And because we live in a globalized world, many of the clothes we buy traveled from halfway around the world. Shipping and delivery leave a huge environmental footprint. Therefore, the cost of an article of clothing is far greater than the dollar amount found on its tag.

False Advertising and the Environment

Fashion is all about image. While the world's concern for the environment has led to some improvements in production processes, the fact of the matter is that fashion conglomerates must still try to meet demand. Companies try to juggle economic realities and consumers' preferences for green goods. This has led to a lot of false advertising. Many companies are guilty of marketing a green product but not doing the work of making their products truly sustainable. This phenomenon is known as greenwashing.

Yet many artists in the industry bring widespread attention to these issues. Eileen Fisher is the face of the movement to produce sustainable clothing. Stella McCartney and Ralph Lauren join her in reforming the fashion world. Though these names are just a few, they model a commitment to sustainable goods. While big companies continue to greenwash, there is still an opportunity for consumers to "vote with their dollars" by shopping at stores that put our planet first.

Humanitarian Issues

When we think of health issues, we think of cancer and other maladies, not the chemicals that potentially cause them. Carcinogens, parabens, lead in the water, and other poisons are currently a sad fact when it comes to manufacturing. Often it seems that corporations are under no obligation to be transparent about how their products harm your health.

Just as the making of clothes causes pollution, wearing synthetic garments can pollute your body. Fashion involves a lot of chemistry. Whether dyeing a textile or finishing a handbag, the garments we wear and carry every day have gone through many chemical processes. The Center for Environmental Health has found lead and other hazardous materials in garments from fast-fashion chains. Many of these companies are still selling lead-contaminated pieces—accessories especially. Belts, purses, and shoes can potentially expose shoppers to chemicals associated with health issues. And prolonged exposure to high levels of chemicals can have serious consequences. For example, infertility, heart attacks, strokes, and high blood pressure are all associated with lead exposure.

Of course these ill effects can also affect the people working in factories that make garments. Historically, humanitarian issues have plagued the fashion industry. Between health issues and bad labor practices, the industry has a lot of room for improvement. Child labor is another cause for major concern.

When we look at a gorgeous garment covered in beads or sequins, we don't often think of the person who might have hand-stitched them onto the fabric. Sadly, when you see beads or sequins on a garment, there's a high likelihood that that work was done by a child. Beading machines are very expensive, and it's rare that an overseas manufacturer would spend the money on one. And so beadwork is often done by children off the books. The International Labour Organisation has shown that about 260 million children are employed around the world. Fast-fashion is a large reason why these children are working tirelessly to meet the market demands.

Uzbekistan, for example, is one of the top cotton producers in the world. Young children can be seen collecting cotton during the summer months as mandated by the government. Children can be threatened with expulsion from school if they do not perform the tasks assigned to them. Unfortunately, this is just one of many instances of unethical labor practices in the fashion industry. Many factories around the world are associated with limited educational opportunities, dangerous equipment and conditions, and even slavery. And these labor issues don't just affect children. Many of the workers in the fashion industry are women. They are often underpaid and exposed to hazardous chemicals and other pollutants.

Most of us don't know where our clothes come from. Even if we know the location of a manufacturer's headquarters, we cannot readily trace where a garment's fabric was made. And so, unless a company is transparent, every purchase we make potentially furthers these unethical labor practices.

It's more and more important to take even just a little bit of time educating ourselves about the places we buy clothes from. The internet is a great resource for finding organizations, like the Fair Labor Association, that shed light on manufacturers' processes. Forbes even releases a yearly list on their website called "The World's Most Ethical Companies."

DESIGN to CHANGE the WORLD

As we've learned time and again from great artists, art can be a catalyst for change. Fashion is no exception. Leaders in fashion design are blazing new trails in the industry that address labor and environmental concerns. These innovators demonstrate that art and invention go hand and hand—and can change our world for the better.

Eileen Fisher

Eileen Fisher is one of the world's biggest fashion designers. She is from Des Plaines, Illinois, and currently lives in New York City. Inspired by the simple kimono, Fisher's fashion is also known for its simplicity. She designs pieces intended to last women for the whole of their life.

Fisher is a champion of sustainable design practices. Despite the fact that fashion is the number-two pollutant in the world and Eileen Fisher Inc. is one of the world's biggest names in fashion, Fisher received an environmental award from Riverkeeper for her sustainable methods of production. Fisher's company has switched the cotton they use in clothing to organic cotton. In fact, 84 percent of the cotton used in Fisher's designs is organic. (And 68 percent of linen used is organic, too.) Fisher's goal is to be a fully sustainable supply chain by 2020.

Her company-wide initiatives address human rights, environmental sustainability, and consumer rights. Fisher's silks are not dyed using hazardous materials. The transition to organic cotton and linen is part of a larger goal of abandoning rayon entirely. Fisher's team is looking into new fabrics with safer chemistry, new versions of polyester, and recycled fabrics. This means better use of fabric scraps on the cutting room floor but also letting consumers bring back Eileen Fisher clothing items to the store so they can be reused or recycled.

Fisher champions human rights. Her employees all over the world are considered part of the brand's family. The company has trained workers to voice their concerns and advocate for their own rights since Fisher Clothing's start. Fisher pays fair-trade wages to all workers. In India, she launched The Handloom Project to invest in and empower rural weavers. Her leadership addresses broad concerns with practical, achievable modes of change.

FASHION CULTURE

Fashion is everywhere. It's always been a part of popular culture. But ever since iconic figures made certain fashions trendy and instantly recognizable—from James Dean in a leather jacket, to Marilyn Monroe in that white dress, to Beyoncé Knowles in a Roberto Cavalli gown in her visual album *Lemonade*—there has been an increasing understanding of fashion's ability to shape culture. The rise of fashion has led to more spaces for designers to express themselves.

Project Runway

Project Runway is a television series in which contestants compete to design the best clothes. Each episode poses a different contest. At the end of each contest, a panel of fashion's most elite arbiters of taste decides whose garment was the best and whose garment sends them home. In the end, two or three designers get to have a runway show during New York Fashion Week, culminating in a final winner.

Project Runway has been on television since 2004. The reality television show has given hope and

Project Runway judges Tim Gunn, Heidi Klum, and Michael Kors

94 Inventions in Fashion: From Rawhide to Rayon

The Future of Fashion 95

GEORGINE RATELBAND

Not all rising stars have to make it through the tough competitions of reality TV. Twenty-five-year-old Georgine Ratelband has already made a splash in the fashion world, just two years after launching her first line. Born in the Netherlands, then raised in Belgium, Ratelband draws inspiration from her extensive travels in many of her pieces. When she was a design student at Instituto Europeo di Design, her thesis collection was purchased by a Belgian boutique. Her first fashion line was so good it premiered at New York Fashion Week in 2014. Ratelband mixes classic tailoring with all kinds of textures. By understanding the science and math behind these various fabrics and time periods that inspire her, she's been able to rebrand femininity as a mix of the urban (tailoring and wearability) with the glamourous—the eye catching.

Ratelband, so far, has created multiple dress styles. Instead of describing them by silhouettes as most designers do—A-line, empire, shift, tunic, drop waist—she describes them in terms of female empowerment. Ratelband cares about the feeling that the clothes evoke. Ratelband's passions for travel, art collecting, dinner parties, and the like are evident in her choices of fabric, theme, silhouettes, and colors, season by season. Her work has already been worn in fashion features for *Elle* in Indonesia, *W* magazine, and on celebrities—Anne Hathaway, Beyoncé, Ellie Kemper, Kylie Jenner, Gabrielle Union, and Taraji P. Henson, to name a few.

inspiration to young designers everywhere. By watching people from all over the country (many of whom do not yet have careers in the field) build garments, viewers understand the labor and art that should be at the center of the industry. Further, it gives people a glimpse at the struggles and excitements of being an artist in New York City. The host, Tim Gunn, serves as a mentor to these budding designers. The show's accessibility gives young people who might not have a background in fashion design an idea of what it might be like to attend the Fashion Institute of Technology, design their own line, and style models on the runway.

FASHION'S BRIGHT FUTURE

From the time of rawhide until now, fashion is an industry that has grown substantially. At the beginning, we were a species figuring out what tools could help us better survive than other species. We've come a long way from those bone needles and loincloths in prehistoric times.

During the 1900s, the world saw two horrible wars. They changed everything about our day-to-day lives. Fashion designers, like many other innovators and artists of the time, took it upon themselves to reflect the changes in the world by offering clothes that matched new attitudes and ways of life. This vision of Western fashion has been seen in mainstream art and design ever since that dark time in the world's human history.

Now, globalization is upon us, bringing us all kinds of new challenges and changes. Our humble objects, like cotton, continue to be a source of conflict in many lands across the globe. It will take a whole new crop of artists and inventors to make what we wear on our backs sustainable and life giving. Will it be the 3D printer that gives us a new way of producing textiles with less manual labor? Will a designer bring us clothes from closer to home than the labyrinth of textile trades? Only time will tell.

GLOSSARY

aniline leather Stained leather that has not been treated with a pigmented finish.

awl A small, pointed tool used to poke holes in a variety of materials, especially heavy materials like leather and canvas.

bolls The rounded seed pod of plants, such as cotton.

buffed leather Leather that has been processed with an abrasive cylinder to take the top layer of grain off.

Canadian tuxedo A tuxedo made of denim as first worn in Canada by Bing Crosby, designed by Levi Strauss.

chain stitch An ornamental sewing stitch where loops are crocheted or embroidered in a chain.

chrome tanned Leather tanned with chromium salts, resulting in a light blue color.

crusting The final processes of leather tanning in which leather has been tanned, dried, and dyed, but not yet finished.

denim A sturdy cotton twill fabric used for jeans, overalls, and other clothing.

drawing plate A hardened steel plate with various-sized holes through which wire is pulled to make it consistently thinner.

eye-pointed needle A needle used on a sewing machine in which the point and eye are on the same side.

filament A slender, threadlike object or fiber found in animals and plants.

grain The surface pattern of animal hides after hair or fur has been removed.

hide Outer covering of a fully grown animal made up of three layers.

indigo A dark blue dye cultivated from a tropical plant.

leather Hide or skin that has been tanned for human use.

lint The fibrous material of a cotton boll.

lockstitch A stitch made by firmly linking two threads or stitches together using a sewing machine.

pre-shrinking A process invented by Levi Strauss and Co. to insure that denim would not stretch after multiple washes and wears.

rawhide An animal hide which has been treated for preservation, but not yet tanned.

sammiering The process by which water is pressed out of hides.

suede The velvety result of buffing leather with an abrasive surface.

vegetable tanning Leather tanned with water extracts from plants and no other chemicals.

warp In weaving, the lengthwise threads that the weft thread crosses to make cloth.

weft In weaving, the term for the thread which is drawn through the warp yarns to create cloth.

BIBLIOGRAPHY

Brasch, Nicolas. *The Industrial Revolution: Age of Invention.* New York: PowerKids Press, 2014.

Carlson, Laurie M. *Queen of Inventions: How the Sewing Machine Changed the World.* Brookfield, CT: Millbrook Press, 2003.

Cavendish, Richard. "The Singer Sewing Machine is Patented." History Today, August 21, 2001. http://www.historytoday.com/richard-cavendish/singer-sewing-machine-patented.

Charleston, Beth Duncuff. Based on original work by Harold Koda. "Christian Dior (1905–1957)." *Heilbrunn Timeline of Art History.* New York: The Metropolitan Museum of Art, October 2004. http://www.metmuseum.org/toah/hd/dior/hd_dior.htm.

"The Cotton Gin." Eli Whitney Museum. Retrieved June 11, 2016. https://www.eliwhitney.org/7/museum/eli-whitney/cotton-gin.

Fontaine, Mia. "The History of Denim." Zady, November 16, 2014. https://zady.com/features/the-history-of-denim

Forsdyke, Graham. "A Brief History of the Sewing Machine." International Sewing Machine Collectors Society. Retrieved June 12, 2016. http://ismacs.net/sewing_machine_history.html.

Hackett, Robert. "A Brief History of Blue Jeans." *Fortune*, September 17, 2014. http://fortune.com/2014/09/18/brief-history-of-blue-jeans.

The History Channel. "Cotton Gin and Eli Whitney." History.com, 2010. http://www.history.com/topics/inventions/cotton-gin-and-eli-whitney.

"History of Parchment." Kare Parchment. Retrieved June 14, 2016. http://www.parsomen.com/history_of_parchment.htm.

"History of Sewing Needles." Sewing Mantra. Retrieved June 9, 2016. http://www.sewingmantra.com/index.php/needles/history-of-sewing-needles.

Koda, Harold, and Andrew Bolton. "Paul Poiret (1879–1944)." *Heilbrunn Timeline of Art History*. New York: The Metropolitan Museum of Art, September 2008. http://www.metmuseum.org/toah/hd/poir/hd_poir.htm.

Krick, Jessa. "Charles Frederick Worth (1825–1895) and The House of Worth." *Heilbrunn Timeline of Art History.* New York: The Metropolitan Museum of Art, October 2004. http://www.metmuseum.org/toah/hd/wrth/hd_wrth.htm.

Lipka, Mitch. "Bamboo-zled: FTC Says Retailers Fibbed About Bamboo Product Claims." AOL.com, February 3, 2015. http://www.aol.com/article/2010/02/03/bamboo-zled-ftc-says-retailers-fibbed-about-bamboo-product-clai/19343673/?gen=1.

"The Manufacturing Process of Rayon." Textile Exchange. Retrieved June 18, 2016. http://www.teonline.com/knowledge-centre/manufacturing-process-rayon.html.

Miklosic, Galina. "A Short History of Manufactured Fibers." Fiber Source. Retrieved June 19, 2016. http://www.fibersource.com/f-tutor/history.htm.

Morris, Ernest. "Rawhide Braiding: History in California." Preserving the Vaquero Tradition. Retrieved June 14, 2016. http://elvaquero.com/rawhide-braiding.

"Nordstrom, Bed Bath & Beyond, Backcountry.com, and J.C. Penney to Pay Penalties Totaling $1.3 Million for Falsely Labeling Rayon Textiles as Made of Bamboo." Federal Trade Commission. December 9, 2015. https://www.ftc.gov/news-events/press-releases/2015/12/nordstrom-bed-bath-beyond-backcountrycom-jc-penney-pay-penalties.

"Rayon." How Products Are Made. Retrieved June 20, 2016. http://www.madehow.com/Volume-1/Rayon.html

Stewart, Jude. "The Simple, Humble, Surprisingly Sexy Button: A Visual History." *Slate*, June 14, 2012. http://www.slate.com/articles/life/design/2012/06/button_history_a_visual_tour_of_button_design_through_the_ages_.html

"Stitches in Time: 100 Years of Machines and Sewing." Museum of American Heritage, June 4, 2004. http://www.moah.org/virtual/sewing.html.

Wright, Jennifer. "The Complete History of Blue Jeans, From Miners to Marilyn Monroe." *Racked*. February 27, 2015. http://www.racked.com/2015/2/27/8116465/the-complete-history-of-blue-jeans-from-miners-to-marilyn-monroe.

FURTHER INFORMATION

BOOKS

Beaton, Cecil. *The Glass of Fashion*. Garden City, NY: Doubleday & Company, 1954.

Dior, Christian. *The Little Dictionary of Fashion: A Guide to Dress Sense for Every Woman*. New York: Abrams, 2007.

WEBSITES

Heilbrunn Timeline of Art History
http://www.metmuseum.org/toah
This website pairs essays and works of art in a chronological history of art. While this extends to multiple visual art forms, it includes costume and fashion design, especially as an art form of global culture.

Leather Resource
http://leatherresource.com
This site takes you through the many processes involved in tanning and making leather, focusing on practices from the leading tanneries in Italy and Brazil—two countries whose leather goods are still coveted today.

Sewing Mantra
http://www.sewingmantra.com
Sewing Mantra is a forum for sharing information about sewing and related industries. The forum allows professionals and amateurs to communicate. The blog features articles about the history of sewing, needles, thread, and the like.

INSTITUTIONS

American Textile History Museum
http://www.athm.org
This museum is located in Lowell, Massachusetts. It explores the art, history, and science of textiles. The exhibits and collections of the museum depict movements in human history based on discoveries and developments of textiles all over the world.

The Costume Institute
http://www.metmuseum.org/about-the-met/curatorial-departments/the-costume-institute
The Met has a specific institute dedicated to costumes from all parts of human history. With over thirty-five thousand garments, these works span over seven centuries of fashion in human history.

INDEX

Page numbers in **boldface** are illustrations. Entries in **boldface** are glossary terms.

acetylation, 67, 69, 70
A-line waist, 20
aniline leather, 31
appropriation, 87–88
Audemars, Georges, 69–70
aviators, 5, 34
awl, 22, 56

back strap loom, 22, **23**
beamed, 42
beret, **16**
blue jeans, 7, 38, **40–41**, 88
 invention of, 45–46, 48–49
 legacy, 50, 52
 reception of, 49
 technology that led to, 39, 42–45
bolls, 43, 72
Bolsheviks, 34
bomber jackets, 34
bone needles, 7, 24, 55
boots, 7, 32, **33**, 38, 56, 64
Brando, Marlon, 36, 50
bright pink, 17
buffed leather, 31
buttons, 5, 7, 17, 39

caftan, 14
Canadian tuxedo, 50
cellulose, 67, 69, 70, **71**, 71, 72, 73, **72–73**, 75, 78, 80
chain stitch, 56, 57
Chanel, Gabrielle "Coco," 15, **16**, 17, 18, 20–21, 86
Chanel No.5, 18, **19**
Chanel suit, **16**, 18, 20
Champs-Élysées, **10**
Chardonnet, Hilaire de, 70, 71
chiffon, 18
child labor, 90–91
chiton, 14
chrome tanned, 31
clothing bans, 6
collagen, 30
corset, 14
cotton gin, 6, 39, 42–44, **43**
couturier, 11
cowboy, 24, 32, 34, 38, 46, 48, 50
Crosby, Bing, 59
crusting, 30, 31

Dean, James, 50, 93
denim, 7, 21, 45, 48, 50
dermis, 30
digital textile printing, 84
Dior, Christian, 20, 83
Doge, John Adams, 57

draping, 14
drawing plate, 55
Dreyfus, Camille, 67, **68**, 69, 71
Dreyfus, Henry, 67, 71
Duncan, Scott, 56
Dupont, 81

embroidery, 23, 56
epidermis, 30
Exposition Universalle, 12
eye-pointed needle, 55, 56, 57, 60

fast-fashion chains, 90, 91
felt, 21
filament, 73, 74
Fisher, Eileen, 89, 92–93
flappers, 17
Fonzie, **35**, 36
fur, **27**, 28, 29, 30, 36, 37, 55

gauchos, 24, 32, **33**
Gore, Robert, 79
Gore, Wilbert, 79
Gore-Tex, 79, 81
grain, 30, 31
Great Depression, 74
Great Exhibition of London, 12
Greece, 28, 32, 42
Greenough, John, 57

greenwashing, 89
Gunn, Tim, **94**, 97

H&M, 9
Happy Days, 34, 36
harem pants, **13**, 14
Hart, William, 50
haute couture, origins of, 11–12, 14
hazardous materials, 90, 91
Henderson, James, 56
hire-purchase system, 64, 65
House of Chanel, 17
House of Worth, 12, 17
Howe, Elias, 45, 57, 60
Hunt, Walter, 57

immigrant labor, **53**
indigo, 39, 42, 49
Industrial Revolution, 22, 44, 54, 62
Inuits, 27–28, **27**, 55

jersey, 15

kimono, 14, 92
Klum, Heidi, **95**
Knowles, John, 57
Kors, Michael, **95**

lace, 7
lampshade tunic, 14

Index 109

leather, 5, 7, **33**, 24, **35**, 56
   how it's made, 29–32
   iconic uses, 32, 34, 36
   legacy, 36–38
   tanneries, 21, 25
leather jacket, 5, 34, **35**, 36, 50, 93
Levis, 48, 49, 50, 52
Levi Strauss Museum, 52
lint, 43
"little black dress," 18
Livescribe Notebooks, 84, **85**
lockstitch, 57, 60
looms, types of, 22

Madersperger, Josef, 56
"Manus x Machina," 86, **87**
milliner, 15
Misfits, The, 50, **51**
Monroe, Marilyn, 50, **51**, 93

Native Americans, 29
Naudin, Laurent, 67
"New Look," 20
nylon, 38, 69, 74, 80, 86

parchment, 28
Paris, 11, 12, 14, 15, 17, 20, 21, 24, 70
parka, **27**
Pasteur, Louis, 70
patent leather, 34
Pergamon, 28

petticoat, 14
pochoir, 14
Poiret, Paul, 12, **13**, 14, 17
pre-shrinking, 49
Project Runway, 93, **94–95**, 97
pulp mills, 75

Ratelband, Georgine, 96
rawhide, 24, **26**, 28, 31, 88
   how it's made into leather, 29–32
   iconic uses, 32, 34, 36
   invention of, 29
   legacy of, 36–38
   precursors, 25, 27–29
rayon, 21, 66, 81, 88
   invention of, 69–74
   legacy, 75, 78–80
   reception of, 74–75
   technology that led to, 67, 69
Rebel Without a Cause, 34, 50

Saint, Thomas, 56
sammiering, 31
seamstresses, industrialization's impact on, 6
sewing machine, 7, 21, 23, 85, 88
   early machines, **58–59**
   invention of, 6, 45, 55–57, 60, 62

legacy, 64
reception of, 62–64
technology that led to it, 54–55
Shivers, Joseph, 81
shoulder pads, 17
shuttle, 60, 62
Shützenberger, Paul, 67
silk, 21, 22, 66, 69, 70, 73, 74, 75
Singer, Isaac, 55, 60, **61**, 62, 63–64, 65
Slater, Hannah Wilkinson, 22–23
slavery, 44, 91
software, for fashion design and styling, 84, 85
spandex/lyrcra, 80, 81
Stone, Thomas, 56
Strauss, Levi, 46, **47**, 48, 49, 50, 52
subcutaneous layer, 30
suede, 31
Swan, Joseph, 70
synthetic fabrics, 66, 80, 81

tailors' uprising, 63
Teflon, 79
textiles, early, 21–22, 25
Thimmonier, Barthélemy, 57, 62, 85
thread rolls/spools, 22, 23, 24, **67**

3D printing, 85–86, 98
  objects made using, **82**
tools, early, 22, 25
treadle, 62, 64

Urban Outfitters, 9, 88
Uzbekistan, 91
vaquero, 32, **33**
vegetable tanning, 31
Velcro, 45
vellum, 28
Vogue, **4**, 18
Vuitton, Louis, 36

warp, 48, 49
Wayne, John, 50
weft, 48, 49
Whitney, Eli, 42, 43–44
Wiesenthal, Charles Fredrick, 55–56
Wild One, The, 36, 50
World War I, 15, 17, 50, 69
World War II, 20, 34
Worth, Charles, 11–12

yarn, 22, 48, 69

Zara, 9
zippers, 7, 17, 39

Index 111

ABOUT the AUTHOR

LISA HITON is a filmmaker and poet from Deerfield, Illinois. She was a costumer for her high school theater department, run by the divine Susan Gorman, where her first job was to be a milliner making hats from scratch for *Arsenic and Old Lace*. She's been a part of the wardrobe department for many plays and films since. She went to film school at Boston University and has a degree in arts in education from Harvard University. She teaches poetry, film, and literature at universities on the East Coast.